'Who, Sir? Me, Sir?'

K. M. PEYTON

'Who, Sir? Me, Sir?'

OXFORD UNIVERSITY PRESS
OXFORD TORONTO MELBOURNE

Oxford University Press, Walton Street, Oxford OX2 6DP

Oxford   London
New York   Toronto   Melbourne   Auckland
Kuala Lumpur   Singapore   Hong Kong   Tokyo
Delhi   Bombay   Calcutta   Madras   Karachi
Nairobi   Dar es Salaam   Cape Town

and associated companies in
Beirut   Berlin   Ibadan   Mexico City   Nicosia

Oxford is a trade mark of Oxford University Press

British Library Cataloguing in Publication Data

Peyton, K. M.
Who Sir? Me Sir?
I. Title
823'.914[F]   PR6066.E/

Typeset by Rowland Phototypesetting Ltd,
Bury St Edmunds, Suffolk
Printed in Great Britain by
Biddles Ltd, Guildford, Surrey

I

It was their own form-master Sam Sylvester who got them into the trouble in the first place. Raving Red Sam Sylvester had a bit of a chip on his shoulder about the status of the Hawkwood Comprehensive (the Gasworks, as it was known locally, owing to the highly progressive architecture which featured a lot of ventilation pipes) compared with the elite Greycoats Independent down the road. Nobody else cared about it, were pleased, in fact, to co-exist with such splendid aggro material so conveniently to hand. When it came to slanging matches against Greycoats the Gasworks were well ahead on points; in examinations and suchlike boring rubbish the Gasworks were quite happy for Greycoats to take precedence.

'They've only got twelve in a form, sir,' Deirdre McTavish – better known as Nutty – pointed out the obvious reason for this last coincidence. 'If you only had twelve of us instead of thirty-two you'd manage much better.'

'You'd be able to keep order, sir. I mean, it's not enough to fight back really, twelve.'

'Thank *you*,' said Sam with some asperity.

If it were to come to a physical fight with Nutty McTavish he doubted if he would win, for she was a formidable thirteen-year-old with a fighting spirit unmatched by any of her male counterparts in the class. She had tough parents to match, but an elder sister Gloria of such melting tenderness and charm that left one confounded by the biological processes. Nutty forebore to compete in the charm stakes. She flaunted her facial disasters – a broken nose, thick pebble glasses and wireworks on her teeth – with disarming unconcern. Her large grin and knotted black curls were, strangely enough, more memorable. But you treated Nutty with care.

5

'You lot – your trouble is – you lack ambition!'

Sam was apt to come out with explosive, inconsequential damnations which his class bore patiently, sympathetically.

'What do you want us to be ambitious *in*, sir?'

'In achievement. In *wanting* –'

'Wanting what, sir?'

They knew he wasn't articulate enough to say; liked to see his thin face suffuse with frustration, enjoyed his suffering on their behalf. It was kind of him. They liked him.

'To better yourselves.'

How touching, they thought.

'But you haven't, sir,' Hoomey pointed out.

Hoomey, a transparently innocent, completely unmalicious, undersized, earnest child was given to state unpleasant truths out of pure honesty. He was sensitive, vulnerable, amazed when his honest truths gave offence. He saw Sam wince.

'I'm trying, Rossiter. Believe me, I'm trying. But you – the lot of you – you drag me down, because you are so *apathetic*. I can only achieve through *your* achievements. I want so much for you, and you want nothing for yourselves.'

They sighed collectively and rolled their eyes.

'For instance, what do you want in life?'

'Who? Me, sir?' (Hoomey had achieved his nickname by his surprised habitual reply at any address aimed in his general direction.)

'Yes, you, Rossiter.'

'Nothing, sir.'

'You see.'

Nutty's hand shot up.

'Yes, Deirdre?'

'I want to win the junior at Wembley and be selected for the junior team for Brussels and then go into seniors and win the world championship at seventeen and be selected for the Olympics before I'm twenty-one.'

'That's better,' Sam said.

'I jolly well will too. The first bit anyway. The rest depends on Dad getting me a decent horse.'

6

'From Uncle Knacker,' Preston said.

'Why not then?' Nutty flashed her belligerence at Preston.

Her uncle was a slaughterman who had given her an animal on its way to the abbatoir. Her father, a greengrocer, had stabled the pony behind the shop in the middle of town, fed it on sprouts and boiled potatoes and encouraged Nutty to turn it into a show-jumper. The results had been phenomenal. If you knew about show-jumping, you had heard of Nutty McTavish, even seen her on television in replay when there was a lull in the senior event and the commentator decided to fill in with earlier happenings. She had days off for Hickstead and her mother sent a note to say, 'Deirdre has her bilius attack and won't be coming in. Thank you. Yours truly, Mrs McTavish.'

Getting the general idea off Nutty, Hoomey put his hand up. He was always willing.

'Yes, Rossiter? You want –'

'To go and watch Northend United.'

'Your life's ambition?'

'Yes, sir. On Saturday.'

'What's stopping you?'

'Oh, er – getting there, sir.'

'It's only seven miles away, the ground. Haven't you got a bike?'

'It's got a puncture, sir.'

'There's a bus.'

'It doesn't stop by my house, sir.'

'It stops at The Red Lion. About a mile and a half from your house.'

'It's too far, sir.'

'God give me strength,' Sam said.

'Yes, sir.'

'I'll take you, in my car. Would you like that?'

'Oh, yes please, sir!'

'You and three friends. That's all I can fit in. I will call for you, at the door, on Saturday.'

'Oh, thank you, sir!'

Which is how it all started.

2

Hoomey took Nutty, Nutty's cousin Bean (son of Uncle Knacker) and a Sikh boy called Jazz, an amiable lad in jeans and a turban who lived down the road from him. Nutty insisted on coming; Hoomey didn't ask her. She just said to him, 'I'm your friend. Count me in,' which brooked no argument. The game was good. Hoomey enjoyed it, his spirits only moderately dashed on the way home by Sam's pointing out that his life's ambition was now fulfilled.

'Twelve and three-quarters, and nothing more to aspire to. You lucky young toad!' Sam crashed his gears down to second as his decrepit car met a slight hill. Jazz, whose father drove a Mercedes, winced and held on to his seat.

'I'll try and think of something else, sir,' Hoomey said brightly.

'You do that, lad. I'm stopping at the Red Lion for a pint. You lot want cokes, crisps?'

'Yes please, sir.'

The Red Lion was on the outskirts of town, in 'the country' – if so it could be called – where fields showed coyly between pre-war semis, sprouting electricity sub-stations and pylons, drive-in garden centres and the odd cow or two. Uncle Knacker owned three fattening fields between two arterials half a mile down from the 'Red Lion'. The publican at the Red Lion was Sam's girl-friend's brother-in-law, a popular man whose large carpark was usually well-filled. Sam parked his Mini alongside a smart Volkswagen bus with 'Greycoats School' painted in high-class italic lettering along its side.

'There you are,' he said. 'You can uplift your minds in cultured conversation while I get my drink.'

There were four boys in the van, drinking cans of coke.

'We don't want to talk to *them*, sir,' Bean said.

'Try it amongst yourselves.'

8

'Oh, funny.' When he had gone Nutty said, 'He's always *saying* things.'

'Sticks and stones may break my bones,
   But words will never hurt me,'
Jazz quoted. 'My mother taught me that. She read it in a magazine. It's an old English saying.'

'Very useful for you,' Nutty said, knowing how Jazz got ragged, mostly for his turban. Not that he got annoyed very often, being flexible by nature and well-primed by his parents. 'I don't like being got at. Sam's always getting at us.'

'He's all right,' said Hoomey.

Sam brought them out a coke and a bag of crisps each and went back inside.

'I mean,' Hoomey said, 'I mean, after all –'

'Yes, all right, I know. But he gets at you. Wants you to be –' Nutty paused, not quite sure what he wanted them to be, but knowing that he wanted them to be something other than they were.

'What?' said Hoomey.

'Search me. Ambitious,' he said.

'To achieve,' Jazz said. 'He said to achieve.'

'What've they achieved then?' Bean asked, jerking his thumb at the Greycoat neighbours.

'Cokes, like us,' Hoomey said.

'We've achieved crisps as well. We're up on them.'

'If I was Sam, I'd want to achieve a better car,' Jazz said. 'I'd like a big car, a big house and lots of money.'

'I think the idea is we're supposed to want all those things and work hard to get them.'

'I knew there was a snag in it,' Hoomey hooked round in his crisp bag for the last crumbs. 'Count me out.'

Nutty, staring hard at their neighbours, said, 'That blonde one, with the big hooter, he's called Sebastian Smith. He goes out with our Gloria.' She pressed her nose to the window and gave him a wave. Sebastian gave her a frosty look and returned to his coke. Nutty wound down the window and said, 'Sebastian! It's me, Nutty.'

9

Sebastian wound down his window and said, 'Get lost.'

'That's nice! What you doing here then, nice boy like you, hanging round the pubs? Label on your car and all, parked outside the Red Lion. At least we haven't got a label, telling the world.'

'That car doesn't need a label. You've only got to look at it – Gasworks standard. Goes without saying.'

'You been to the soccer?'

'We've been competing.'

'What in? Ladies' bowls?'

'Tetrathlon. You wouldn't know. Long word of Greek origin.'

'What is it? Three-legged thousand metres?'

'All round athletics. Running, swimming, shooting and riding cross-country.'

'You have to do all four things, or a choice?'

'All four. It's very demanding, for high-class athletes. You wouldn't understand. Very competitive.'

'Where'd you come? Bottom?'

'First, out of twenty teams.'

Sebastian wound the window up on this good note, terminating the conversation.

'Jeez,' said Bean. 'I feel tired.'

'Very tiring watching soccer,' Hoomey agreed.

'I bet I could do that,' Nutty said.

'Do what?'

'Tet- whatsit. I can do all those things. Not shooting, but any fool could learn that. Hey, Seb!' She leaned over and knocked vigorously on the window. Sebastian opened it two inches. 'Do they have girls?'

'No.'

'Why not?'

'They're too weak for it.'

He shut the window again. Nutty took off her glasses, crossed her eyes and pressed her face hard against the glass, aiming at Sebastian's superiority. He smiled, wound the window down and said, 'Did anyone ever tell you your sister's much prettier than you are?'

'I've got the brain,' Nutty rapped.

'Just as well. You've got a lot to make up.'

'I hate that Sebastian,' Nutty said, shutting the window hard. She flung herself round, back to the Volkswagen, but the door catch went and the door swung open with a crash against the bus. Nutty flew out backwards, hitting her head hard against the Volkswagen door panel.

'Bloody hell, look what you've done.' Sebastian got out and came marching round with his friends to inspect the damage. There was a large dent in the panel and a scratch in the paint. Nutty was groping round for her glasses, moaning.

'I can't see. Where are they? Don't tread on them.'

'What are we going to say to old Plumpton? Bus damaged by girl's head. Sounds weird. I say, what's this I'm crunching underfoot?'

'*No!*' Nutty flung herself blindly at the opposition. 'They're not broken? Please!'

'Calm down. Only bent. No worse than the bus. This door looks like a double decker bus hit it. How come you're still conscious?'

'Because I'm a *girl*. I've got grit and stamina. Give me my glasses.'

'Thick. Solid between the ears,' said one of Sebastian's friends. 'Stands to sense, like a battering ram.'

Hoomey and Bean held Nutty down, quick to act. 'Cool it,' Jazz said, grinning, knowing the feeling.

'Should've been you,' Hoomey said. 'All that padding. Let's get back in before they come back. With luck no one'll notice.'

They parted to their respective cars and waited, somewhat anxiously. Sam being a long time, Bean went to investigate and came back shaking his head. 'Him and that Plumpton, fraternizing. Sam's had about ten pints by the look of him. Waving his arms about.'

'He loathes Plumpton.'

'Arguing.'

In another ten minutes Sam and Plumpton came out together.

They walked briskly over to the two cars and Plumpton bent down and peered in through the windows of the Mini.

'This lot, you mean?'

Nutty wound the window down and smiled in a civilized fashion.

'That's a girl,' Plumpton said.

'Quick on the uptake,' Bean said.

'No girls,' Plumpton said to Sam. 'Girls are out. That leaves you three. By Jove, and one of them's a –' He hesitated.

'A darkie?' Sam prompted, amused.

Plumpton looked embarrassed. 'Well – I mean, it looks odd, dammit. But there's nothing in the rules against it.'

'He's British. Aren't you British, Singh?'

Jazz agreed that he was, in his best Indian accent. Usually he spoke native urban Essex, identical to his friends'. The others all fell about.

'You'll want another,' Plumpton said to Sam.

'No difficulties there.'

'I'll discuss it with you then, when I've seen the committee. I think it's damned sporting of you, given the material you've got to work on.'

'It's a deal,' Sam said. He and Plumpton shook hands. The seven boys and Nutty stared at them suspiciously.

'Cheers then.'

'Cheers, old man.'

Plumpton climbed into his bus without a glance at the damage and drove off. Sam followed, only detained by trying to shut the door properly, which took some time.

'What's all that about, sir?' Hoomey asked.

'I'll tell you on Monday morning, Rossiter, when I've got things sorted out a bit. Very interesting. Very profitable. I'm very glad I went into the Red Lion.'

They watched him curiously, shaking their heads.

'Did you *achieve* something, sir?' Bean asked.

'Very good, Bean! I did indeed! I'll tell you all about it on Monday, in class events. Something to look forward to.'

They weren't so sure, but made no comment.

3

On Monday morning Sam came to class events with dark
shadows under his eyes, looking ten years older over a weekend.
He came to the door with Foggerty the games master, who was
grinning like an ape. Nutty, coming in late, heard Sam say, 'Look,
I made a bet and I'm going through with it. We attempt *nothing* in
this school, and even if I've bitten off more than we can chew
here, it's better to try –'

'And fall flat on your face?'

'You're jumping to conclusions.'

'If you'd handpicked them, you idiot – but that crew! Does the
head know?'

'Yes he does. And I'm counting on your support, Foggerty.'

'My support! You want prayer and fasting from the sixth form
down to get anywhere –'

'All right, you've made your feelings quite clear.'

'In the Red Lion, you said? How many pints had you – ?'

'That's nothing to do with it. It was a challenge. I couldn't
stand by and take it from that arrogant old blimp without putting
a word in.'

'A good too many words, I reckon. You're out of your mind,
old fellow. But I'll stand by you, never fret.'

'Thank *you*.'

Nutty went to her seat, intensely curious. Sam knocked over
his jar of biros on his desk, gathered them up and dropped his
notebook. He sat down carefully, went through the day's essen-
tial business, then locked his fingers firmly together on the
table-top.

'I have something very important to say to you today. I want
you to listen carefully. I have taken it upon myself to enter into a
challenge, which – at first hearing – may seem a quite impossible

challenge. It concerns certain members of this class, four to be precise, but it will, if it is to stand any chance of success, require the support of every one of you, of every one in the school, in fact. I intend to rally that support. Some people think I am attempting the impossible, but I have enormous faith in the latent potential unexploited in this school.'

No one in his class understood what he was talking about. Nutty had an inkling, but couldn't believe it. Hoomey, in the next desk, was yawning, having sat up late to watch the horror film, and had a comic open on his desk which he was reading whenever his eyes happened to be open. He heard his name mentioned, repeated. He focused on Sam with difficulty.

'Who, sir? Me, sir?'

'You, Rossiter. And Bean, and Singh.'

'What, sir?'

'I have accepted a challenge laid down by Mr Plumpton of Greycoats School that this school will field a tetrathlon team against his own team, good enough to really give them a run for their money, if not to beat them. For those who do not know what tetrathlon means, it is a combination of four sports: running, swimming, shooting at a target and riding across country. Hawkwood will produce a team, train hard for a year and compete against Greycoats next summer. The school will provide the training and also the horses. The Headmaster has agreed to the idea, and so has the chairman of the Parents Association. I trust that you too will consider the idea worthy of a modicum of enthusiasm.'

His gaze rested on Hoomey, who smiled encouragingly.

'I think it's a very good idea, sir.' He wondered how many pints Sam must have imbibed to come up with it. Sam looked pleased and surprised. Nutty leaned across her desk and said, 'Dear Hoomey, take that grin off your face. I think Sam means you.

'What do you mean?'

'You, in the team. That's what I mean.'

Hoomey looked at Sam, not believing it. Sam was smiling. Hoomey opened his mouth, but found that he was speechless.

Nutty obliged for him. 'The team consists of Hoomey, Bean and Singh – is that right? Not me because I'm a girl. Because we were in the car on Saturday, when you met Mr Plumpton?'

'That's right, Deirdre. Mr Plumpton has the odd notion that his pupils are in some way superior to Hawkwood's. I said that *any* Hawkwood boys could beat him, given adequate training. It is the facilities we lack here, not the human calibre. That is the point I want to prove. We take *any* four boys, and we concentrate on providing them with first-class, intensive training, and my contention is that we can produce a team in every way as competitive as Greycoats'.'

The class stared back at him, awed by his optimism. Even Nutty felt that the obstacles to be overcome in the Hawkwood path were something in the nature of the Grand National course. Hoomey's mouth was opening and shutting like a goldfish. There were so many reasons he could think of that stood in the way of his emulating Sebastian Smith of Greycoats that he could not start to list them. Even the irrepressible Bean was silent.

Preston was brave enough to spell it out. 'This huntin', shootin' and fishin' lark, sir, they can't do that. It's unnatural. Running and swimming perhaps. But even then, Hoomey can't swim. And Singh 'll get waterlogged.'

'Can't you swim, Rossiter?' Sam looked shocked.

'A quarter of a width, sir.'

'Hmm. Well, you'll have to work hard at swimming.'

'I can't ride either. Or shoot.'

'You'll have to work hard at riding too. And shooting,' Preston said. 'It only leaves running and, if I were you, I'd start now.'

Hoomey, desperate, said, 'I've got a weak heart, sir.'

'You haven't, Rossiter. Faint heart, perhaps – a mental condition. But physically – this type of exercise will do you the world of good. Build you up.'

'Gasworks Mr World,' Judd said.

'Oh, jeez! It's not fair!'

Nutty gave him a daggers look. 'You are a *weed*, Hoomey! I'd take your place any day. Sir, can't I be in the team? I was in the car too.'

'I'm sorry, Deirdre, but the teams have to be male. If it were possible, I would include you.'

'No one would know, sir,' Preston said.

'You've still got to have a fourth member. There have to be four. You could include Preston.'

'Mr Foggerty agreed to produce the fourth. Someone good at running and swimming. All the riders in the school appear to be girls, so unfortunately we will have to train from scratch in that department.'

'They'll never do that in a year, sir,' Nutty said. 'Five years more like.'

'You might be able to help, Deirdre. Even if you can't be in the team, your enthusiasm is commendable. In marked contrast to that of Rossiter, Bean and Singh.'

'They'll come round to it, sir. I could be captain, sir. You know, they have captains – Olympic teams and that. Could I be? It's not fair, if not, just because I'm a girl. I was in the car, after all. Part of the random sample. It's owed to me, really, to be in the team. I wouldn't mind captain.'

'Possibly, Deirdre. We'll discuss it. There will be a lot to discuss later. I just wanted the idea to be put to you all as soon as possible. It's a very exciting project and one that could really prove what we are capable of when we try.'

'When Hoomey, Bean and Singh try,' Preston corrected. 'I think it's splendid.'

'Hoomey, Bean and Singh don't,' said Bean bleakly.

'Hoomey, Bean and Singh are lumbered,' Preston said.

The bell went and Sam stood up, smiling happily. They could see that he was genuinely moved and excited by his insane idea. He truly did think they were capable of coping with this looney sport. When he had gone, pandemonium broke out.

'Gasworks for gold! Good old Sylvester!'

'We'll cheer like mad for you,' Preston promised. 'Bring our picnics and watch you all day. It'll be great. I think it's a great idea.'

Surprisingly, this was the reaction of the whole school. After the first incredulity, the fact that nobody actually had to do anything but encourage Hoomey, Bean, Singh and the unknown fourth member went down very well. The weight of encouragement was sufficient to work miracles.

'After all, you can do anything if you try hard enough.'

'It's only practice. And hard work.'

'It's not a gift, or anything. Only get the training in. Anyone can. Sam's quite right.'

'Just get good people to work on you.'

'To show Greycoats – it'd be great!'

'Smash them! They're so bloody superior –'

'A little weed like Hoomey – to show 'em. It'd be terrific! It's a great idea!'

Sam, having introduced the snowball, saw it start rolling without any more help from him. The fact that it was such an audacious ambition fired the imagination.

'If he'd proposed a team of our best athletes, it would have been interesting, encouraging, no more.' Mr Howarth, head of English and dabbler in psychology, interpreted the mood in the staffroom. 'But to go out on a limb and take any bunch of morons, just those that happened to be around when he met Plumpton, and propose that they should do this thing – that's really sticking your neck out. It's presumptuous. It's outrageous, in fact. That's what people like about it, the enormity of the challenge.'

The headmaster chewed his lips anxiously. 'It's *got* to work, if we go ahead with it. We can't afford to be annihilated. Beaten by a short head possibly, but decimated, no. And it will cost money – the training. We shall want specialists for the shooting and the riding. The cost of the horses . . .'

'Mr Bean has undertaken to supply the horses,' Sam said. 'And the Parents Association is going to raise funds. They've got a jumble sale under way already. They are very keen, sir. Enormously so.'

'The material, Mr Sylvester – what does Mr Foggerty say about the potential of those boys? They aren't the ones I would have chosen. That little Rossiter, he doesn't strike me as having the courage. An amiable lad, but lacking spirit. Bean – yes, possibly, more spirit there and I understand his father likes the idea. There will be family backing – no doubt the McTavish branch will be muscling in on the act, if Deirdre is to act as captain. Is this wise, by the way?'

'I think so, sir. She has colossal drive. It's a great pity she can't be included. And she should be valuable on the riding side. This sport, you understand, is run by the Pony Club, and Plumpton tells me he can arrange for us to enter their unaffiliated competitions without actually getting too involved. He doesn't think there will be any complications there.'

'Oh, great heavens, Sylvester, the Pony Club! The tweed and wool stockings brigade. The ladies are really formidable. We shan't have to get involved with all that?'

'No, sir, only as far as the actual competition, which they organize. I don't think you need worry.'

'I'm not quite sure what we're letting ourselves in for, Sam. You've got me worried. And the Sikh boy, that's another thing. We'll have crash-helmet trouble there with the horses, just like the motor-bike contingent – the least of our troubles, I daresay. What do his parents think about it?'

'I'm not sure, sir. He hasn't said anything.'

'He might do well. He's got backbone, that boy. More brains than the other two. Who is the fourth member of your team, Sam? Who has Mr Foggerty suggested to you?'

'Well, sir – I'm not sure whether it's a good thing, the boy being so unreliable, but he wants Nicholson, sir. He's the school's best swimmer and he can run as well.'

'He needs to, that boy, considering how often the police are after him. It's very unwise. He's likely to be in borstal by next summer.'

'I said that much myself to Mr Foggerty. But Foggerty says something like this might do him a lot of good. He says he's bored.'

'Yes, I've heard those theories myself. We'll mug a little old lady to relieve the boredom. Well, a bit of tough training will prepare him for borstal if nothing else. Sam, seriously, this has got to work, you know. We can't afford to be made fools of.'

'No, sir. I have complete faith, else I wouldn't have suggested it.'

His voice trembled slightly, but he didn't think the head noticed.

4

Hoomey couldn't accept the awful thing that had happened to him. He weighed himself on the bathroom scales. Six stones, six ounces. Seventy pounds. Thirty odd kilos. He had always skipped swimming because he got teased about his bones sticking out. Ribs like a xylophone, they said. Play us a tune, Hoomey. Is there a woodpecker in the changing room? No, it's Hoomey shivering. He just didn't look the right sort of boy – in the bathroom mirror he saw his wishy-washy face, freckled and slightly spotty, his wishy-washy blue eyes staring mournfully back; in no way did the image relate to the brown, sparkling athletes who drank beer after a game of soccer in the commercials. He was droopy and small for his age and his joints stuck out at knees and wrists and elbows as if he was waiting to grow into them, like clothes. He was perfectly happy that way, or had been up to now, but it wasn't a body to put to competition. Sam must have been out of his mind.

'Your tea's ready, love,' his mother called up the stairs.

He went down slowly. His knees clicked when he went up and down stairs. Perhaps he could get a doctor's certificate, to say it would do him a damage.

'Fancy you being in this team then,' his mother said to him fondly. 'Look, I've got you a bit of steak. Start building you up.'

She put a plate of steak and chips down on the kitchen table with an array of sauce-bottles and vinegar. The kitchen was small and cramped, the house having been built pre-war with a dining room which you were expected to eat in. There was a dining table in there but it was never used for eating from.

'It's awful,' he said to his mother. 'The team, I mean, not the steak. I can't do all those things.'

'No. But they say you're going to get trained. Really first-class training. Brigadier Somebody-or-other, and an army boxer.'

'Who says?'

'Mr O'Malley of the Parents' Association. I was talking to Mrs Bean in the hardware this morning. Everyone's full of it, you know. They all say it's time Hawkwood was put on the map against that Greycoats. They say Greycoats is always in the newspapers for winning this and that. It'd be nice to give 'em something to think about.'

'This other team we've got to beat – we met them on Saturday. They're top out of twenty teams.'

'Greycoats team? Who are they then?'

'Sebastian Smith. Antony Royd. I know them. Two others – Colin Constable and some gink called Fountains Abbey or something.'

'Fountains-Abbott? His father's a magistrate.'

'Someone for Nicholson to beat then. They've probably met.'

'Mark Fountains-Abbott. I used to clean for his granny, old Mrs Fountains-Abbott, before I married your dad. And that Royd – he'll be Doctor Royd's boy. He sings in the choir at St Peter's.'

'Well, they can all do this stuff already. Ride and shoot and that.'

'So will you, dear. It's only opportunity. That Antony Royd, I remember, Mrs Royd was expecting at the same time as Mrs Bean had Kevin, and he was premature. Only four pounds.'

'Well, he's grown since then.' Antony Royd was going to look like a beer advert in another year or two, coming into the bar from the polo-field or getting out of his powerboat after a race. He had strong wrists and a charming smile. Hoomey couldn't think of him at four pounds.

'How big was I?'

'Seven and a half.'

20

It helped, somehow. If he beat him then, at birth, he might do it again.

'Mrs Bean says you've got to join the Pony Club. Have they told you anything about that? It comes under their rules or something?'

'Oh jeez. Who said?'

'Mrs Bean said Mr Bean said.'

'But they're – they're –'

Hoomey stopped, the sauce-bottle in mid-air, words failing him. He had seen them at the County Show, where he had gone for the rabbits, all those girls with plaits and scrubbed faces and clean gloves, doing an exhibition ride. They had scornful eyes and superior expressions and were all called by sensible names like Susan. Nutty said they were ghastly. She said they did everything in teams, for the honour, and what was the good of that, when she could leave them all standing with one arm tied behind her back?

'They're what, dear?'

'You know,' he said helplessly. 'You *know* –'

'No, dear. I always think they look lovely at the show.'

That was it really, he thought gloomily. Him and Nicholson were never going to look lovely, however hard they tried.

'I'm going down Bean's,' he said, despairing.

Bean was a boy of wit and resource, and might find a way of deliverance. His mother was obviously surprised, for he rarely went out, moving no farther than to the chair in front of the television set.

'You can practise running,' she said brightly.

'*Ugh*!'

He tried it, crossing the corner of the demolition site, but it made him cough. If this thing was really on, he might have to pack in smoking. He slowed down and scuffled across the bus-stop kicking a brick. Their house was on the main road coming uphill out of the town centre. A few fields were just starting to leaven the bricks and mortar, but were mostly full of thistles, earmarked for building. There was a council estate behind them where Bean lived. He made for it, taking a short cut

21

through the carpark adjoining a few prefabricated sheds that called themselves the Hawkwood Industrial Estate. Behind was a large expanse of grass, nettles, old barbed wire, bricks and oil-drums. The housing estate was on the other side. Across the open space one could look down on the town, a busy, self-important place boosted in the last few years by highrise office blocks full of income-tax men and VAT clerks. Hoomey could see the glass towers against the line of the estuary beyond, looking ethereal in the evening sun, like Indian palaces, save they had no knobs. The pier had knobs but was derelict, entry barred since the last fire. Nicholson was reputed to have had something to do with the fire. Hoomey frowned, thinking about Nicholson. He always avoided Nicholson, who scared him. Gary Nicholson was what Hoomey's mother called a nasty rough boy. His elder brother, Nails, still at school, played water-polo for the town and stole cars. Their father was a builder and their mother had run off with an Irish bricklayer. 'Keep the social workers in full employment, that lot,' Hoomey's father said often. 'They're what the rates get spent on, instead of education and drains. People like that should be –' His wife always cut in here. 'Now, Alan, don't say what you don't mean. We'd all be as bad as Stalin if we did some of the things you suggest.' In fact Alan Rossiter was a very mild-mannered man, not a bit like Stalin. Mr Nicholson, Hoomey thought, was a bit like Stalin. Having a Stalin for a dad must make you turn out like Gary and Nails. Hoomey's father was a VAT man.

The Bean family was large and noisy and much under the thumb of father Bean, Nutty's 'Uncle Knacker', a fierce fat man with silver hair and a red face. Hoomey did not care for him much. Mrs Bean was fat but not fierce, very placid in fact, and cheerful. She thought the idea of young David being in the Gasworks tetrathlon team really great. Young David, eating his tea, gave Hoomey a look in which Hoomey recognised the same despair as he felt himself.

'Got the horses coming tomorrow,' Uncle Knacker barked. 'The Parents' Association coughed up – used the money they'd got in the sports fund. Five hundred quid for the four. Stands to reason you don't get much for that sort of money, but I done well, I reckon. Ex-chasers, and one out of a circus down on its luck. Jumps through hoops. All you got to do is duck.' He clumped Hoomey on the shoulder and roared with laughter. Hoomey felt sick.

'Chasers? What do they chase?' he asked apprehensively.

'Good God, boy, the horse in front. Old race-horses, over the sticks. Can jump like stags.'

Hoomey felt faint.

'Have a cup of tea, love,' Mrs Bean said comfortably, pouring it.

'I – thought – ponies –' They'd said the *Pony* Club, he thought. Not the Jockey Club.

'You want jumpers, mate, and jumpers you're getting. We won't let you down, trust Knacker Bean. I said to your headmaster, "You can trust me, mate," I said, and he said, "Mr Bean, you're my man," he said. "I won't let you down," I said. "We think it's a great idea." '

'Everyone thinks it a great idea,' Mrs Bean said happily.

Not everyone, Hoomey thought, but did not demur. He escaped with Bean from the tea table as soon as possible and slipped out of the house, heading back for the open spaces of the industrial estate. Hoomey, from feeling miserable, now felt downright scared.

'I don't want to ride a racehorse!'

'They're clapped out,' Bean said. 'Probably won't move. What sort of a racehorse d'you think you get for a hundred quid? That's not even carcass money.'

Hoomey stopped and looked at him. 'You sure?'

'Course I'm sure. My dad probably got them for fifty each, if he said a hundred. No need to be scared, only they might drop dead on top of you.'

Hoomey felt better.

'Where are we going to keep 'em?'

'Here, Dad said.'

'Here?'

They were standing on the waste ground behind the car park

which Hoomey had crossed on his way to Bean's.

'Handy, Dad said. He's borrowed one of the warehouses to use as stables. The old refrigerator factory.'

It didn't seem quite natural to Hoomey, but he didn't comment on the fact. None of it did.

'We'll go and tell Jazz, shall we?'

'Okay.'

They kicked an old can across the weedy ground, heading for the Singh home. Mrs Singh made things like enormous crisps called pompidoms, or somesuch funny name, and Hoomey was spurred on his way by the thought of them. The Singh home intrigued him because although Jazz – apart from his looks – was as normal as himself, once in his own house he took on a sort of foreign ambience, changing subtly into an Indian to fit into the undeniably different atmosphere. It always fascinated Hoomey, the differentness. At school, he wasn't different at all. He was two people, School-Jazz and Home-Jazz. Hoomey had remarked on the phenomenon once and Jazz had assented. 'Well, I have to. You go along with 'em.' Hoomey wondered who he would go along with when the day came his parents arranged his getting married, for Sikhs arranged it for their sons, Hoomey knew. He thought of Jazz being presented with a cross-eyed, spotty, knock-kneed, gook-speaking bride from the Punjab and having to go along with that. He wanted to ask him, but didn't dare. Save that all Indian girls were pretty, so it might be a nice surprise. Might even be very trouble-saving, to have it all done for you. Only the idea made his mind boggle. He never said any of this to anybody, only thought it sometimes. He got on quite well with Jazz.

Jazz's father was a taxi-driver and drove a big diesel Mercedes, which was now parked outside the house. The house was a neat Victorian villa in a row with lime trees outside; Hoomey liked the road better than his own; it was cosier, somehow, with the trees and the privet hedges and its back to the sea. Jazz's house always had a funny smell, a foreign smell. Hoomey knocked on the door and looked through the letter-box, and the smell came out to him. Mrs Singh came down the hall and opened the door, smiling.

'Come in.'

She was plump and short and always wore Indian clothes, sometimes with a cardigan on top. She never said much, but smiled a lot. Hoomey thought she didn't speak English very well; she spoke Punjabi to the family, but Mr Singh always spoke English and Jazz only spoke gook to his mother, not to anyone else. Jazz was watching the television. He never wore his turban at home, which always gave Hoomey a jolt of surprise, seeing the knee-length black hair coiled on top of his head, skewered in place with a comb. His hair was the one major battle that Jazz had failed to win with his parents; Jazz wanted to cut it, but uncut hair was a dogma of the Sikh religion and Jazz couldn't win.

'Wait till you have a bloody beard and all,' Hoomey had sympathized with him on occasion, for Mr Singh had a large beard secured under his turban. Hoomey marvelled at this, in fact thought it rather splendid, but could see that the prospect was unlikely to excite Jazz.

Mr Singh was eating his supper, which looked very peculiar, all brown, and smelled delicious. He grinned at them happily.

'What's this about running and jumping and racing about then? Jaswant says he's in team with you?'

'That's right.'

'You not happy either?'

'Not really, no.'

'I think it fabulous! We come and watch. Very fine for school.'

'Yes,' Hoomey lied.

'On horse?'

'Some of it, yes.'

'Jaswant's great grandfather great horseman. I tell him, it will come easy. Great Grandfather great warrior in army, on horse.'

Jazz groaned.

'How come it'll rub off on me? Your father was chief cook to the Maharajah of Patiala or somewhere but I can't boil an egg.'

It was extraordinary how all the parents were so keen, Hoomey thought. Even old Stalin Nicholson might be exhorting Gary this very minute, over egg and chips, recalling his days as fastest hod-carrier in the high-rise development before the lumbago got him. All very fine for *them*, Hoomey thought, all fat and

25

run to seed, rejoicing in the dreadful honour that had befallen their sons.

Jazz switched the television off and came outside with them and they kicked a tin-can round the field a bit and then sat on some dumped oil-drums and watched the lights come on along the front and smoked a cigarette and reflected on their fate.

'Our last free night,' Bean said. 'The horses'll be here tomorrow. Dad says we've got to start on them at once.'

'Mr Foggerty's taking us to the baths after school, he said.'

'This Brigadier Harris or whoever is bringing the guns at lunchtime.'

'We can shoot ourselves,' Hoomey said.

'They only kill rabbits,' Bean said.

When Jazz was in bed, lying staring at the strange patterns the lime-tree leaves, illuminated by the lamp-post, made on his bedroom ceiling, his father came up to him, moving softly round the door.

'You still awake?'

'Yes.'

'I found you something.'

He put the light on. Jazz rolled over on one elbow, blinking.

'I look all evening, through the tin trunk, and I find him. Your great-grand-father. You put him on bedside table and he inspire you. I put this little light on, and you see him. You pray you will be like him and all will be well.'

He turned off the main light switch and put on the bedside lamp, and against the lamp he propped an old brown photograph.

'You keep him here, and say your prayers, and all will be well.'

'You're joking,' Jazz whispered.

'You have no faith.'

'No.'

'You getting English, no good.'

Jazz did not reply. His father went out, leaving the small light on. Jazz reached out for the photograph and held it, examining it

26

closely. It showed an old Sikh warrior on a pony, glaring at the camera fiercely, a huge spear in his hand. Behind him in the dust lay a dead tiger. Jazz looked at it for a long time, then he propped it back against the lamp, and turned the light out.

He didn't know whether to laugh or cry.

5

The next day Mr Foggerty told the four boys to meet him at the Town baths after school.

'But we've got to go and help with the horses. They're coming tonight, Mr Bean said.' Hoomey's tone of voice indicated that his strength would not be equal to two extra-curricular excursions in one day.

Nutty said, 'The horses won't come back till Uncle Knacker leaves work. They won't be home till about seven. Plenty of time.'

They scowled at her. Mr Foggerty said, 'Quite right, Deirdre. That's settled then.'

'We haven't brought our things,' Jazz said.

'I'll provide things.'

Nutty grinned. 'I'll come too, as your captain, That's okay by you, Mr Foggerty?'

'Yes.'

'You louse,' they said to her, when Mr Foggerty had gone.

'Jeez!' She rolled her eyes. 'You're so *keen*! I'm going to dope your school dinner.'

'It's illegal for athletes.'

'Who's talking about athletes?'

'How far have we got to swim for this competition?' Gary Nicholson asked.

'As many lengths as possible in four minutes. I was talking to Seb about it and he says he does eleven. That's in a twenty-five metre bath.'

27

'*Eleven?*' Hoomey had to sit down. He thought suddenly of Antony Royd, weighed in at four pounds, doing eleven lengths in four minutes. It wasn't possible! He felt tired all day, just thinking about it. On the way there, he said to Nutty, 'It's not going to work. I shall die.'

'Good. I'll be able to take your place.'

Some captain, Hoomey thought! Tactful, encouraging, a tower of strength to lean on. Perhaps Nutty had second thoughts along the same lines, for she then said, quite nicely for her, 'You only think you can't do these things, Hoomey. If you start trying you might surprise us all. How do you know?'

'I do try.'

'No. But I shall make you.' She spoke very seriously, not joking at all, and her eyelids dropped down over her weirdly magnified eyes, thinking about trying, how she had tried, how she still tried to make her pony, Midnight, win. How she had worked at it, evening after evening since she was nine, learning to ride, learning to jump, falling off, hurting herself, carrying on doggedly with Uncle Knacker shouting at her. And now she knew that Uncle Knacker didn't know any more than she did, and she was on her own because her parents couldn't afford expensive lessons or a top-class pony. If she was going to qualify for Wembley, she was going to have to do it on her own and Midnight just had to be good enough. She got up early to muck him out and groom him and exercise him, and she babysat nearly every evening to keep him in good oats (not Uncle Knacker's) and shoes, and when she saw the riders she was up against in the collecting ring, with their adoring parents and their fat cheque-books, it just made her all the more determined to beat them, because determination was all she had. Midnight did it because she willed him to, because she slaved to keep him up to it. When she looked at poor little Hoomey, she was filled with pity for him being so hopeless.

How queer she looked sometimes, Hoomey thought, watching her. He supposed it was merely what those awful specs did to her eyes, but sometimes she had an almost maniacal look of purpose in her face, not like a little girl at all. Just as well she had such guts really, because no one was going to love her for her feminine self.

28

She needed guts to face always being passed over by the boys for her gorgeous sister Gloria. He was terribly sorry for her, being how she was, but supposed they all had their cross to bear, like Jazz being coloured, and Gary having Stalin for a father.

Gary was the only cheerful member of their party, the swimming baths being his familiar habitat. (Wait till later, when we go up to Uncle Knacker's, Hoomey thought.) His brother Nails was already there, terrorizing the deep end, but came out when he saw them and hung around – presumably to find out how awful they were. He was small for a swimmer, thin and lanky and pale-skinned. He had pinkish freckles and spiky blond eyelashes, and eyes redrimmed with too much chlorine. In spite of his apparent insignificance, he was hard and dangerous and insolent; he had virtually no friends at school, but hung around after school with older boys known as 'a bad lot'. The staff at school loathed him, but found his genius for getting into locked cars undeniably useful whenever they lost their car keys, which seemed to happen quite frequently. Gary, although a born lawbreaker, was nicer natured than his brother, and was known to laugh and smile on occasions. Nails only laughed if anybody had an accident or hurt themselves.

'Clear off unless you want to be useful,' Nutty said to him.

She looked like a tank in her bathing costume, Hoomey thought, squat and powerful and belligerent. She couldn't see without her glasses, which made her frown with frustration. Jazz was frowning too, from natural inclination, mostly at having to wear a bathing cap, which he hated.

'They all wear them in the Olympics,' Nutty pointed out. 'It cuts down the friction.'

'You'll do twenty lengths to my fifteen,' Hoomey said.

All right for Jazz, cap or not, for his dark body had a natural grace and he could swim far better than anyone had suspected. Mr Foggerty was agreeably surprised, but when Nutty reminded him of the standard required, he relapsed into grim gloom and stood on the side of the bath in his white T-shirt and jeans looking at his watch and saying, 'I can't spare the time to do this three nights a week for the next year, which is what is required. The

29

mind boggles, Miss McTavish. Mr Sylvester is up a gum tree.'

'You've got to,' Nutty said doggedly. 'Somebody has anyway.'

Her eyes peered towards the deep end, where Nails was holding his brother down and the lifeguard was getting worried. (Hoomey hadn't got in yet.)

'He's here every night,' she remarked.

'Nails, you mean?'

'Yes.'

'Nails is hardly my idea of a dedicated, encouraging, competent swimming instructor.'

'He knows how to do it though,' Nutty pointed out. Having released Gary, Nails was swimming at a phenomenal speed after another victim. 'If you can do something as well as that, you must be able to convey – a little bit –'

'It doesn't follow, girl. Nails is a villain.'

'Perhaps he lacks motivation. Mr Sylvester says we all do. If you motivated him –'

'Where do you learn all these long words?'

'Off Mr Sylvester.'

'How do you motivate someone like Nails? Offer him a set of skeleton keys? A box of gelignite?'

'I bet I could think of something.'

'Think on then, Captain. Because getting young Rossiter up to eleven lengths will see me to the grave. Life's too short. Nails has ten years to spare over me. Slither in now, young Rossiter, and let's see just how bad you are. Let's face the worst.'

Hoomey slithered, abandoning hope, and felt the water close over him like death, and opened his mouth to scream, and started to drown. Nails came unexpectedly and rescued him, hauling him up by the chin and putting the rail under his hand.

'You're a bloody nutcase,' he said to him. 'Use your arms.'

'Demonstrate, Nicholson,' Mr Foggerty said hopefully, but Nicholson demonstrated by swimming away back to the deep end, mostly underwater where he was hard to see. Mr Foggerty, feeling that a good opportunity had just escaped him, got down on his knees and started his lesson. Nutty sat on the edge with her legs in the water, scowling in deep concentration after Nails.

Hoomey achieved his quarter of a width, Jazz did two lengths, Bean three and Gary seven, and Mr Foggerty bought them all a coke each, reminding himself to put it down on expenses, and left them to catch their various buses. Nutty waited with Gary, who said rather ungraciously, 'I thought you lived up Alexander Park?'

'So what?'

Gary and Nails lived in an old dump behind the bus station. Their living room was full of bags of cement, the last she had seen of it. Perhaps Mrs Nicholson had been wise to leave.

'Your brother Nails, what's he do?'

'What do you mean, do?'

'What's his ambition in life?'

'You joking? Keep out of the old man's hair mostly.'

'What's he like doing?'

'What you getting at? He doesn't like going to school for a start, but he goes else the old man beats him up. Me and all. He likes driving cars. Motor-bikes. Down the motorway.'

'Pinching them, you mean?'

'No. Only borrowing. He never does them any harm. He hasn't got his own, you see.'

'He'd like one?'

'Course he would. He'd give his ears for a bike of his own. Who wouldn't?'

'Me,' Nutty said. 'I prefer ears.'

'Well, *you* –' Disparagement was obvious. Nutty was not offended. She studied him objectively, as one of her team, and saw a quite reasonably fit, bright boy, hard with nights of climbing over factory walls and across their roofs and being chased by securicor men, quick-witted out of habit, used to an uncomfortable life. He hadn't the vicious streak that showed in his brother, and might prove a very good team-member. The only one, in fact.

She left him, having found out what she wanted to know, and took her own bus home, mulling over her good idea. Raving Red Sam had ridden a motor-bike once, she remembered, a job that had been much admired by the boys. He had given it up for his very inferior car when he started courting Big Brenda out of the Biology lab – Biological Brenda, as Preston called her, who gave them lessons on sex, and no doubt Sam as well. What had happened to the motor-bike? As Sam himself had taught her, motivation was a great thing. Sam would surely sacrifice a rotten old motor-bike to the cause, in exchange for his team being terrorized into swimming the required number of lengths in four minutes? Nutty thought she was on to a good idea and went home happily, taking over from her mother in the shop as she usually did while her mother started to get the tea. It was only ten minutes, as she had used up an hour in the swimming-baths. After tea she had to ride out on Midnight, which she could work in with going up to Uncle Knacker's to see the new horses. To keep a pony in the middle of a town, and keep him fit, was hard work, as he had to be exercised every day, and the surrounding neighbour-hood was hardly a horseman's paradise. The residential streets didn't like it early in the morning, the clatter of Midnight's hooves on their concrete drives, but she was no worse than the milkman, and they were quick enough to scoop up any free dung for their roses, she noticed. She took no notice – 'There's no *law* against it, mate! Call the police if you like. It won't worry me.' Nor did it, for the patrol men knew her, and her stirrup light was in order.

When the shop shut she went in for her tea. Her sister Gloria was already eating, her hair in rollers. Gloria was officially still at school but took most afternoons off to help in the shop, for which she got paid. She knocked off at half-past four when Nutty got home, and spent two hours in the bathroom getting herself ready to go out, which she did every night of the week. She was good-natured, indolent and highly-sexed. Mrs McTavish used to wonder why she had produced two children who ran to such opposite extremes, but had never come up with an answer. Boys queued up to take Gloria out, but avoided Deirdre, in case she asked them to help her muck out while they were waiting for Gloria to get her false eyelashes in the right place.

'You still see that Sebastian Smith?' Nutty asked her, sitting down to her shepherd's pie, cabbage and chips.

'Sometimes. He's a bit young.'

Gloria was fourteen. 'Immature,' she added. She had a vast helping of shepherd's pie, which she put away quickly and carefully. However much she ate made no difference to her shapely figure. She had very delicate ways and inch-long silver fingernails, in spite of serving in the shop.

'Don't chuck him up,' Nutty said. 'Not for a bit. He could be useful.'

'All right. I wasn't going to anyway. He's very rich.'

'Fine.'

'He's got very nice manners.'

Nutty, remembering her last encounter, couldn't agree, but let it pass. In her mind, determined that her rotten team was going to make good, she was storing away useful data. If they couldn't beat Greycoats by skill, they might stand more chance by guile, and one needed to learn all one could about the opposition.

'D'you know Antony Royd?'

'Mmm,' Gloria nodded through her shepherd's pie, smiling.

'Colin Constable?'

'Mmmm.'

'Mark Fountains-Abbot?'

'Mmmmmmm.'

Nutty raised her eyebrows, impressed. 'Well, keep them all on your list. It might be useful.'

'No sweat,' said Gloria casually.

She swept up her empty plate and took it into the kitchen, and departed upstairs with her cup of tea to start on her coiffure. Nutty sighed, and finished eating, slightly cast down. When she had finished, she went to the mirror, took off her glasses, and fixed on two strips of the false eyelashes that Gloria had left scattered on the table. Without her glasses she couldn't see the effect. She put her glasses back on and the lashes, horrifically magnified through the lenses, curled back at her like gigantic spiders' legs. She blinked, fascinated.

Her mother came in with some stewed plums in a bowl.

'Gloria not want any pudding then?'

'Mum —' Nutty turned round and her mother let out a wild

33

scream, shooting plum juice all over the tablecloth. Nutty scowled, pulling off the glasses.

'You don't scream when it's Gloria.'

'God in heaven, Deirdre! Go and fetch a cloth. Oh, Lord, what a fright! You shouldn't – oh, my word!'

Nutty fetched the cloth and mopped up the table. 'It's not fair. Just because it's *me* –' Her vision was impaired by the gruesome beauty aids, like looking through prison bars, and she picked at them irritably.

'They're stuck.'

Her mother started to laugh. 'Leave all that to Gloria, love. You're much better plain and unadorned.'

'Huh! Plain. Like a tank, Hoomey said. He's one to talk. He's like a toast-rack.'

'Your teeth'll be straight in six months, and you can get contact lenses when your father's insurance comes in at Christmas, grow a bosom and stun them all.'

'I can't get them off.'

'Ask Gloria. Don't do yourself a damage.'

'I'm going up Uncle Knacker's. The horses are coming tonight. I might be late.

'Okay, love. Be careful on those roads.'

Nutty went upstairs and changed into her jods, peeled off the wretched eyelashes and went out to get Midnight. There was a yard behind the shop with an entry off the street; it was cobbled and the stable was where a delivery pony had once been kept. Now Midnight lived a life of luxury, hock-deep in expensive straw, shining and hard and ready to go. Nutty put the saddle on him and set off to meet her team.

6

The cattle-truck moved down the concrete road across the industrial estate and came to a halt beside the knot of boys outside the refrigerator warehouse. Hoomey thought it was like one of those old war films with a bomber coming in to land along a bleak runway and all the ground-crew waiting to know the worst. With the gaunt warehouse and the high vista of derelict open space all round him, he sat on an oil drum, chewing gum. No old bomber pilot, making a forced landing with no wheels, on a load of unused bombs, could possibly have felt as bad as he did at the moment. Jazz and Gary and Bean stood silently beside him. Mr O'Malley, of the Parents' Association, having arrived to see what they had got for their money, stood with the rest of the interested parties, Mr Sylvester and Mrs Bean and Mr and Mrs Singh and quite a lot of the Sports Committee.

Mr Bean got down from the cab, grinning happily.

'Here we are an' all. Quite a reception committee, eh? Just what the doctor ordered! We got plenty to do, turning this lot into stables, an' all. Have a look at the horses first, shall we? Don't get too excited, I'm warning you! The money we got to spend – well, that's the way it is. Give 'em three months on a load of good grub and you won't know 'em.'

The eager parents advanced to undo the ramp.

Hoomey stood up, trying to look nonchalant. His knees felt funny – there really was something wrong with them, he thought, that clicking noise and the way they felt weak. If he were to go to the doctor and ask about it, he might find out –

'Mind yer backs! Mind yer backs!'

An extremely large horse was towing Mr Bean down the ramp. It slithered on to the road, looked round for the nearest tuft of grass and made straight for it, pulling Mr Bean after it. Hoomey happened to be standing on the grass, thinking he was well out of it, saw the horse's great gobbling mouth advancing towards his ankles and leapt back, swallowing his chewing-gum. Speechless, he felt the rope halter pressed into his hand.

' 'E's taken a fancy to you, John mate. Let's make 'im yours, eh? Chose you like, didn't he? That's a boy.'

'*Christ!*' Gary said, staring.

The horse was devouring every clump of grass, thistles, docks, dandelions, sorrel and bindweed that its large upper lip quested upon, clearing the area like a council mower. It was brown, as far as Hoomey could see, and its ribs stuck out like his own, and its great projecting hip-bones were on a level with his head, sticking out like girders as if to hold the gaunt body together. Its legs were knobbled and scarred like old trees, and had some bleeding fresh cuts on them. Its head was aquiline, eyes bloodshot and wary. Hoomey stood paralysed, clutching the rope. The horse, moving to juicier thistles, lifted a great chipped hoof large as a soup-plate and put it down beside Hoomey's plimsoll. Hoomey leapt.

'It could break all your foot like that. It's bloody dangerous,' he whispered. 'Oh, jeez, I don't want it!'

'Yeah, well, you got it, didn't you?' Jazz said. 'Whacko for you. I hope mine's prettier.'

'Circus mare,' Mr Bean grinned. 'Just the thing for you, lad. Make a right pair, you will. Feed 'er up, get a gold lamé turban and you could be back in the ring with 'er no time at all.'

Jazz scowled. Mr Bean's mate was bringing out an extraordinary white horse covered in black spots. It wasn't as large as Hoomey's, but was as thin, and without its companion's extraordinary capacity for ground-clearing. It sniffed at the ground and stood, dejected, motionless. Jazz took its halter. A faint recollection of his great-grandfather's photograph on the quivering, shining, warrior pony came into his mind.

'You don't see one like that every day!' Mr Bean said cheerfully. 'What do you think?'

'Just as well, if you ask me.'

Nutty, unnoticed, had joined the group on Midnight, and sat surveying the new horseflesh without enthusiasm. Her Midnight, gleaming, keen, delicately mouthing his bit with impatience at being asked to stand still, underlined the contrast in quality. She knew it, and said, with the quick tact of the born captain, 'Well, it's what you make of them. Midnight was a pretty tatty beast when we bought him. You can't expect them to be anything *yet*, straight from – well –' Better not underline their intended destination before being deflected by Uncle Knacker.

Gary and Bean were looking understandably nervous by now, their eyes fixed hypnotically on the ramp of the horse-box. Even Mr Bean looked slightly apprehensive.

'Might be a bit of trouble. Keep clear. Bit nervous, this one. Bin in bad 'ands. Needs a bit of lovin', you could say.'

There was a lot of crashing from inside the box, which rocked sympathetically. A shout and a lot of bad language.

'Mind yerselves then!'

A horse came down the ramp in one bound, as if on wings, hit the concrete in a shower of sparks. It wheeled round, took in the scene with dark, terrified eyes, and stood trembling. It was covered in sweat, and was more presentable than the others in looks, but far less so in demeanour. Both Gary and Bean took a step backwards. Even the parents looked worried this time – probably thinking of legal liabilities, Hoomey thought. He felt fanatically encouraged that this wasn't to be his horse. Mrs Bean stepped forward and said, 'You're not giving that to our David.' Her voice was full of authority, and Mr Bean hesitated.

'Gary, it's only frightened because of the journey. It's the best by miles. Take it.' Nutty slipped off Midnight's back, gave the reins to her uncle and went forward and took the creature's halter. She stroked its neck, led it away from the interested crowd and over to the grass. It went in a series of bounds, its eyes showing white, flecks of foam scattering from its lips.

'Poor sweetie,' Nutty said gently.

'Not you. She means the horse,' Bean said to Gary.

Gary was as frightened as the horse. Hoomey thought he could easily start frothing at the mouth, the way his colour had drained. Himself, he felt better and better. His horse was quite normal compared with the other two, only large and hungry, quite acceptable characteristics. He was keeping his feet well out of the way, following where his horse ate. He thought he would soon be out of sight.

'I'll hold it for you,' Nutty said to Gary. 'Don't worry. It'll settle. It's just upset.'

She was the only one encouraged by this choice of Uncle Knacker's, recognising the touch of class she desired. It was the only horse so far which was the right size and the right shape – or perhaps it was only the spots that detracted from Jazz's mount. You couldn't really see the shape of the spots. But this one . . .

'It'll be nice when it's calmed down. You're lucky.'

'I want to live.'

'I thought you liked trouble?' Nutty spoke with some asperity, not encouraged by the marked lack of enthusiasm her team was displaying. God help her, as if there weren't problems enough . . .! The last horse, Bean's own, stood halfway down the ramp, surveying his reception committee with benign, sleepy eyes. He would move no further, his front hooves clamped down hard, his underlip drooping, his tail clamped in. He was a very large, skinny, washed-out chestnut. Nutty, picturing in her mind the agility required of the cross-country performer, ground her teeth with frustration. Sam Sylvester, she thought, you've something to answer for! She glowered at him, but he was chatting up Mrs O'Malley, looking perfectly at ease. It wasn't possible, she thought! Hoomey was being towed along over the field by an animal that was scarcely recognizable as a horse, so thin and sway-backed as it was. Some figures were coming up from the road to meet him, a girl and a couple of boys. Frowning dreadfully, Nutty struggled with her reluctant sight to recognise the faintly familiar figures . . . yes, her sister Gloria and – no, it couldn't be? – yes, it was! – Sebastian Smith and Antony Royd. Spying. The rats! She'd give Gloria a piece of her mind when she got home! Come to laugh, no doubt, and what a splendid opportunity they were being presented with! Grinning as they approached – as well they might! – pretending they were just passing by, brimming with glee, big muscular athletic boys. She had seen them on their expensive horses, swooping across country, confident in the saddle. *Beasts*!

The parents had all departed into the warehouse with Uncle Knacker to 'knock up a few looseboxes'. How and what with, Nutty could not imagine, but that wasn't her department. Morale was her department. She got back on Midnight, in order to look down on Sebastian and Antony, and squared her shoulders. Garry's nervous mare stayed at her side and Gary, perhaps inspired by her example, straightened up and changed his expression from scared to belligerent, which made him look remarkably like his brother Nails. Their adversaries approached, having given Hoomey a hand, geeing his horse up from behind with some hearty arm-waving.

'These your nags then?' Sebastian asked. 'Better keep that one away from the others' – he nodded towards Jazz's spotted beast – 'in case they all catch it.'

Nutty said icily, 'Not *everyone* can afford made horses that do it without any effort on the part of the rider, like yours. My uncle, with his vast professional knowledge of the saleyard, has managed to find four horses which, although in bad condition – and therefore within our price range – are what 'Horse and Hound' calls proven performers. The spotted mare came from Billy Smart's and jumps a flaming hoop suspended at five feet, the chestnut in the horsebox is an ex-hunter who once belonged to the Duke of Beaufort, this one I'm holding has been placed twice round Badminton, and Hoomey's –'

She paused for inspiration and Seb said, 'Won the Grand National in nineteen thirty-two.'

'No, the Cheltenham Gold Cup in sixty-nine, as a matter of fact.' She needled him with such venom from behind her thick lenses that Seb was visibly squashed.

'You're joking?'

'You don't think we'd get just any old horses, do you, for such inexperienced riders? The horses all know the game all right, so we're halfway there, aren't we? Just a matter of getting them fit again, no trouble there. We're not *stupid*, Sebastian, you know. Merely lacking in opportunity.'

39

She spoke with such hauteur and conviction that even Hoomey wondered whether she was telling lies or the truth. Was his old Bones really a Gold Cup winner? He thought only footballers won Gold Cups. Was old Bones the equine equivalent of Manchester United then, fallen on hard times? Footballers grew old and fell on hard times, so perhaps it was the same for horses. But what had she said about badminton? He couldn't see a horse playing badminton. No way did that fit.

'Badminton isn't –' he started.

'Three-day eventing – what Princess Anne does – did –' Nutty snapped at him. 'This mare went clear round the cross-country. Just a matter of getting her fit again, like I said.'

Seb and Antony were looking at the horses dubiously, trying to see past glories and failing.

'Anyway, what are you doing up here?' Nutty pushed her advantage. 'Don't tell me you were just passing by? Come to have a nose, by any chance? Gloria tell you?'

'We came to see your eyelashes, Deirdre,' Antony said in a soft, taunting voice. Nutty let out a genuine snort of rage, nudged Midnight with her heels and rode Antony into a large patch of thistles, towing the Badminton mare with her.

'Clear off! You're trespassing – you too, Gloria, you cow! You wait till I tell Mum!'

They were unequal to her belligerence and departed, giggling.

'Is all that true?' Hoomey asked, when they were out of earshot.

'Well, why not? You can't prove it isn't, can you? Horses like this, they were good once. It's true enough, isn't it?'

Her eyes flashed on him, silencing criticism.

'It's up to you,' she said. 'They're going to laugh on the other side of their faces before they're through.'

It was beginning to dawn on Hoomey that horses like this – surely? – were going to need quite a lot of attention, feeding, brushing and all that stuff. He supposed the Parents' Association would make a rota of some sort, to come up and do it. They were obviously keen, for the sound of activity from inside the refrigerator warehouse was impressive. Mr Bean had bales of straw in the truck which were being unloaded, and hay and sacks of food, and buckets. The parents were scurrying about like ants. Nutty rode into the warehouse to see if it was ready, and Hoomey followed her, towing Bones, who was ready to go wherever the food sacks were going.

Along one wall of the warehouse, four loose-boxes had been partitioned off by old refrigerators pushed together, which made very satisfactory walls. Mr Bean was opening out bales of straw making deep beds. Mr O'Malley brought the hay, and Sam was filling buckets of water.

'Bring 'em in, lad,' Mr Bean said to Hoomey. ' 'E'll think 'e's in paradise.'

The parents stood round proudly as, one by one, the horses were led into their new home. Even Bean's reluctant character, inevitably christened Whizzo, came at the rattle of a food bucket. They nosed at their deep straw, sampled the hay, straddled out their legs and peed, then settled their noses into the food buckets, which Mr Bean and Nutty between them had prepared. The evening light came through the skylights high overhead, glossing the scurfy backs, the sores, the scabby manes, and a soft echo came back from the walls of the vast, bare concrete building of animal content, feeding. Hoomey, for a moment, felt a strange satisfaction at making his old Bones happy. Even the parents had stopped chattering, watching with communal pride the appreciation of their efforts by the reprieved animals. Pleased, they trailed outside, disappeared down the concrete road. Mr Bean started up his lorry, his mate got in, they waved and drove away. The four boys were left with Nutty. It was nearly dark.

'That's it then?' Hoomey said hopefully.

'For tonight,' Nutty said. 'In the morning they'll need feeding again, and mucking out.'

'Who's going to do that?'

'You, of course.'

The boys stared at her.

'They're yours aren't they? Not everyone's so lucky, being given a horse. I'll meet you up here at seven, show you what to do.'

'*Seven*?'

They rolled their eyes, staggered by the news.

'You mean *we've* got to look after them? *We've* got to do it? As well as ride them?'

'Who else, dimwit?'

'But –'

Nutty got back on Midnight, swung round and glared at them. '*I* get up at six every morning to do Midnight. *And* ride him. And in the evening again, feed and muck out. *I* do it, and *I'm* only a girl. So you jolly well be here at seven, else there'll be real trouble.'

And she turned away, Midnight's shoes striking sparks in the darkness, and set off at a fast trot in the direction of Sam Sylvester's semi-detached in Acacia Avenue.

7

'Mr Sylvester, sir!'

It was difficult visiting with a pony. Nutty had manouevred through the rather narrow gate and was trying to keep Midnight from eating a lavender bush by the front door, and his feet out of a rosebed. She had managed to press the bell with the end of her whip. The light went on in the hall and the door opened.

Sam blinked.

'Good God!'

'I won't come in –'

'No, please.'

'But I want to talk to you.'

'Let it graze on the lawn if you like. I'll come out.'

Sam shrugged into his anorak and joined her on the lawn, where Midnight settled happily to graze.

'Nothing wrong? The horses –?'

'No, they're fine. I had an idea though. About the swimming.'
'Mr Foggerty's in charge of that.'
'We thought of delegating. He says he hasn't got the time to spend – they'll need evenings and evenings, far more than once a week. But we thought – well, I did really – that Nails –'
'Nails? You must be joking.'
'No. He would, if you make it worth his while.'
'What are you getting at?'
Nutty paused, trying to marshal her convictions into the right words.
'What you've always said, about motivation. You remember? He would, if you said to him – well, I think he would, if you said, if you teach those boys to swim, we'll give you a motor-bike.'
'A motor-bike?'
'It's what he wants most in the world. And you've got a motor-bike you don't use any more.'
'*My* motor-bike!'
'Yes, well, this is *your* thing, isn't it? We're all making sacrifices, me and Uncle Knacker and the parents and Mr Foggerty and Hoomey and them. It's not asking much, when all this thing is your thing, isn't it? I mean, all your fault.'
'My Triumph Tiger?' Sam moaned.
'I'm sure it would work.'
'God, Deirdre, you're hard.'
'You don't use it anymore. Not with Brenda not liking it and all. You use your car. Motor-bikes just rot if they're left.'
'It'll rot if Nails gets his hands on it.'
'But the job'll be done then. You don't give it him first. You say he can have it when Hoomey and all swim however many lengths in four minutes, whatever many it has to be.'
Sam dropped his gaze thoughtfully to Midnight's teeth tearing at his grass, and knew that his dear old bike was doomed. It was true he had grown out of it now, but it was the beloved relic of his youth. To part with it to Nails would wrench painfully at his inner being; something would die. Or was it dead already, his wild youth? Or had it always been an illusion anyway? Triumph

43

Tigers should belong to boys like Nails, rough and lawless, not hopeless has-beens like himself. He knew, in his heart, that he had always been a little bit frightened of it really . . . opening out the throttle . . . he remembered the feeling of queasiness that had always accompanied that burst of power.

'Yes, Deirdre,' he said meekly.

He could not bring himself to look at her. 'It might not work, your plan.'

'No, well, no results, no bike. That's easy.' Nutty was confident. 'Nothing's lost, if he can't do it.'

She pulled Midnight's head up off the grass, gathered him together and drew him delicately on to the garden path. Sam saw her in the light from the lamp-post opposite, strong and solid, a natural leader of men, the spectacles glinting, wire teeth smiling in triumph. Sam knew she was worth six of him.

'Very well, Deirdre. We'll put it to him.'

'You and Mr Foggerty. Don't say it's my idea.'

'No. As you wish.'

'That's fine, Mr Sylvester. Goodnight then.'

'Goodnight, Deirdre.'

He watched her trot away down the road, red stirrup light shining on Midnight's dark flank.

'Exit Captain McTavish, triumphant,' he murmured, and went out to his shed to lament over his doomed Triumph Tiger under its sheet of polythene.

8

Nails took his usual Ford Escort that night from the parking lot outside the gasworks where the night shift was working, the one he had a key for, and he and Gary went for a drive round the back streets where they wouldn't meet a patrol car, out into the country for ten miles or so and back again.

'This bloke must think his petrol consumption is up the spout,' Gary remarked, looking at the gauge.

'Only fifteen miles. It won't show. He always keeps his tank full. Sometimes I take the brown Austin. Or the red Mini. I do turn and turn about so's they won't notice.'

'If we go home by the industrial estate I'll show you my horse,' Gary suggested.

'*Your* horse? You serious?'

'Yeah. It came tonight. They said it's mine. It's the best.'

Nails laughed, and headed for the industrial estate. He drove very well, his stony eyes fixed on the road.

'You'll never learn to ride! It's a farce, this idea of Sylvester's.'

'Any more than Hoomey'll learn to swim.'

'No.'

'Well, I didn't volunteer, did I? They'll see it's no good and it'll all be forgotten by Christmas.'

Gary, even as he spoke these words, had an uncomfortable vision of Nutty's harsh determination, and felt slightly uneasy. That girl was like a stick of dynamite. *Seven o'clock* in the morning! And he knew he wouldn't dare be late.

'Where then?' Nails asked, as the turning came up.

'This is it. The old refrigerator warehouse.'

The Escort parked neatly outside the big doors. They got out. It was gone midnight, cold and autumnal, and they shivered in their denim jackets. A thick, gold moon was coming up over the sea, glittering on the roofs of the town below them. It was very still. Silent. Nails looked round uneasily.

Gary slid the door open.

'In here.'

The moonlight flooded through the skylights, filling the ware-house with its cold, stern light. The horses were quiet, three of them lying down, only Gary's horse on its feet. Bones and Whizzo stayed where they were, too tired to move, but the spotty mare got up. The two mares moved round their enclosures side by side, Gary's mare still very nervous, her eyes glinting. The boys stood watching. The spotted mare started to eat her hay, but Gary's mare went on walking round, very edgy.

45

'See, she's got far more go than the others,' Gary said proudly.

'She's prettier,' Nails said.

She had a white star, half-covered by a rough forelock, her ears pricked up with fear.

'She yours, really?'

'Yeah. I told you.'

The fact that Nails was impressed increased Gary's new-found pleasure in his horse. They stood together watching her, both of them moved by unfamiliar feelings. Nails, not liking what he didn't know, rejected them, disturbed, turned away.

'Kid's stuff,' he muttered.

Gary, disappointed, agreed.

Nails lit a cigarette, an excuse for staying in the warehouse.

'What you going to call it? She got a name?'

'No.'

'You'll have to think of something.'

'Yeah.'

They leaned against the old refrigerators, scowling into the moonlight. The town hall clock struck midnight. Gary yawned.

'I gotta be back here at seven!'

'Cracked,' Nails said. 'It's all bloody useless.'

'Yeah.'

They trailed outside, stood by the car. Nails could still hear the straw rustling to the restless mare.

'Right load of old nags. They're all up the creek.'

Gary was silent.

They drove home.

9

'Nails, I want you.'

'I 'aven't done anything.'

'I didn't say you had. A little talk – here –' Mr Sylvester looked

46

nervous, Nails would have said. Mr Sylvester, regarding Nails, would have described him as truculent and downright unattractive. He stood with his back to the wall, head up, challenging, his eyes cold and defiant. He was only small but he was wiry, with hard, knotty muscles. He had spots and his hair was cut aggressively short.

'It's an idea we had, about the swimming. Do you go down to the baths every night? Most nights?'

'Most nights, yeah. I gotta pass, 'cause I'm in the team.'

'The polo team?'

'Yeah.'

'This team of mine, who were down there last night, we've got to get them swimming, you know. Your brother and Rossiter and –'

'You'll be lucky.'

'I thought you might help.'

'It's nothing to do with me.'

'Would you like to be involved?'

'No bloody fear.'

'Would you help if you got paid for it?'

'How much?'

Sam sighed. 'You reckon you could teach Rossiter to swim?'

'You mean for money?'

'For a motor-bike.'

Nails blinked.

'For a Triumph Tiger a hundred, to be exact.'

Nails was silent, as if stricken by an affliction. His eyes glittered.

'The idea is, if you get them all swimming – without Mr Foggerty and me, that is . . . if you take the job on, and take them to the baths several times a week – if you teach them to swim, we'll give you a motor-bike.'

'*Give* it me?'

'Well, I reckon you'll earn it.'

'When'll I have it?'

'When they can swim.'

'Swim how well? A length? Ten lengths?'

47

'I'll settle for ten. That includes Rossiter. Ten without stopping.'

'Ten lengths. Then you'll give it me?'

'Yes. I'll put it in writing if you wish.'

'No. If you say. If you promise.'

'I promise. You'll take it on then?'

'I'll give it a try, yes.'

'You're not to terrorize them, Nicholson, you understand? Teach them. If they complain to me, it'll be no go.'

Nails looked at the floor. 'No.' He went on looking at the floor, thoughtful. 'They won't complain,' he said. 'No way.'

Sam flunked telling the team immediately, although he told Nutty. The team had enough on its mind as it was.

'Brigadier Bedwelty's coming today, to teach us shooting, and Miss Gatehouse is coming next week, to start the riding?' Hoomey, wanting to get his facts right, appealed desperately to Sam after assembly. Having been up since six and groomed Bones until the sweat ran (his, not Bones's) he felt as if the day were three-quarters through. He was ravenously hungry.

'No, Rossiter. Brigadier *Gatehouse* is coming to start you on the shooting next week and Miss *Bedwelty* is coming to discuss the riding arrangements today.'

Actually, what she had said on the phone was, 'I'll drop orf and see the little buggers on my way in.'

Sam was as nervous as Hoomey.

'What're they like?'

'You'll see, won't you?'

'You told 'em we're no good?'

'I told 'em – them – you were nothing of the kind. They can find out for themselves.'

'That we're no good '

'That's not what I mean, Rossiter. They will assess your potential capabilities. Do you understand me?'

'No, sir.'

Sam sighed, and decided not to pursue the matter.

48

'You're to meet me in here, the four of you, after dinner, and I will introduce you to Miss Bedwelty.'

They ate their dinner in silent gloom eyeing the clock.

'Have you met her, Nutty?'

'Mm.'

'What's she like?'

'Moustache,' Nutty said.

'Hairy legs?' Jazz said.

'Bony teeth.'

'You can't have bony teeth. Teeth *are* bones.'

'I mean big – you know –'

'Big knockers.'

'No. She hasn't got big knockers,' Nutty said. 'She's big all the way down.'

Hoomey pushed his potatoes to one side, laid down his knife and fork.

'You need it,' Nutty said vehemently. 'Swimming tonight. Running tomorrow. Mr Foggerty said. You got to eat, Hoomey. You're just a weed.'

'I've been all right as a weed for years. I don't want to change.'

'No. Well, we'll see about that.' Thinking of Nails, tonight, she relented. She was nervous about her plan now. They dragged themselves slowly back to the form-room and sat on their desks, waiting. Footsteps along the corridor. They hunched themselves, frowning.

'In here,' they heard Sam say from outside.

The door opened. They directed their gaze on Miss Bedwelty, confirming the worst. Moustache – not terrible, just fluff really, but yes, moustache – healthy cheeks flecked with broken red veins, big strong hands like a man's with big knuckles, hairy wrists. Hairy tweed coat and skirt, and a woolly hat over thick white hair, cut straight round at ear length, with a fringe. Like an Old English sheep-dog, Hoomey thought, save that her eyes showed, and they weren't doting and soft and brown, but ice-blue and sharp as needles. They went through him and out the other side, and he felt the frost wither his insides, like an early runner bean. He stood up, breathed in steadily, coughed.

49

'Hmm,' she said.

Like being X-rayed, Hoomey thought. Perhaps she would notice his bad knee, discard him.

'None of you ridden before then? Just this gel here?'

'No.'

'By Jove, we'll have to put some time in then!' Her gaze lingered on Jazz, but she was too well brought up to let any doubts show. Jazz's dark inscrutable eyes could well be hiding – Hoomey thought – a far more justifiable amazement at the figure before him. Jazz gave little away, and was not given to complaint. He was happier about the horses than Hoomey, possibly happier about the whole thing, although unlikely to admit it. Hoomey found he looked to Jazz for support, trusting his judgement.

'I'll have you down at my place, try you out, see what's to be done. When can they come, Mr Sylvester? After school?'

'Not tonight, Miss Bedwelty, they're going swimming. Tomorrow Mr Foggerty is taking them running. It will have to be after the weekend.'

'Monday,' Nutty decided.

'Very well. You'll bring them over. At four, say. Wear jeans and lace-up shoes – proper ones. No plimsolls. I can supply hats.' She glanced at Jazz again, showing doubt this time, but not admitting it. 'We'll see what you're made of.'

With this daunting remark she departed. Mr Sylvester went with her, glad to escape the inevitable recriminations, to leave Nutty to her unenviable job as captain. Nutty, cutting short criticism, switched bravely to the swimming awkwardness.

'Nails is going to take you tonight. Swimming. You're to go down there with him after school.'

'Nails! *Nails?*'

Miss Bedwelty was forgotten instantly. Looks of mere truculence gave way to genuine alarm.

'Why Nails?'

'He's got the job. Swimming instructor. He knows how.'

Hoomey felt his stomach swoop horribly. The news scared him rigid.

'He – he –'

'He what?' asked Gary belligerently.

'Oh jeeze!' said Hoomey.

'He'll help you, idiot,' Nutty said, her asperity prompted by her own very reasonable doubt.

'He'll *make* me –'

'Well, somebody's got to!' Tact gave way to native fury. 'You gutless, hopeless bunch of Gasworks layabouts! You weak-kneed, imbecile, spineless –'

She carried on at some length, and felt better for it afterwards. But they just looked sad.

Nails met them, looking as morose as themselves. It was raining and they travelled on the bus in silence. Nutty, very worried, wondered what Nails' strategy would prove to be. But only time would tell. Perhaps he didn't know himself. With his cropped bony head hunched into the shoulders of his badge-covered leather jacket, a grubby towel under his arm, he looked an unlikely trainer, nothing like the smooth Mr Plumpton. Nutty had seen Plumpton training, in white, well-creased trousers and blancoed trainers, his muscly brown boys shooting up and down the baths like automatoms. She sighed. Stuck out her chin. Hoomey could bloody well suffer, if it yielded results. He needed to; it was doing him a kindness, putting iron into his backbone. For his own good. She felt better, convincing herself.

Nails' strategy turned out to be simple: if you put a non-swimmer in deep water it would turn into a swimmer through mere self-preservation.

'Get in,' he said to Hoomey.

'Not here. It's the deep end.'

'You bloody well get in here and swim to where you can stand up.'

Hoomey turned to run. Nails grabbed him, locked his bony arms round the shrinking body and jumped in with him. Nutty, watching, stifled a scream, looking for the lifeguard. He was in his little office, smoking a cigarette. Hoomey surfaced, Nails beside him.

'Bloody swim!' Nails bawled in his ear. 'Or you'll die.'

Hoomey's arms threshed out in agony. Nails turned on his back and glided ahead of him, watching him, waggling a big toe under Hoomey's chin.

'C'mon, you bloody twit, or I'll bloody beat you to pulp!'

Hoomey tried, not wanting to die. Every time he felt himself sinking, Nails' prehensile toes grasped him by the Adam's apple and lifted his head clear of the water. He swam, keeping up with Nails' feet, gulping, coughing. He felt his lungs collapsing, his pulses thundering, his heart failing. Nails' foot hooked for him, picked him out of the water and, with a neat thrust to the chest, stood him upright. The water was halfway up his ribs. He looked round and found himself three-quarters of the way down the bath. He couldn't belive it.

'Not bad,' Nails said casually.

He tottered away across the bath to Jazz and Bean, leaving Hoomey clinging to the rail, gazing down in amazement at the distance he had swum. Nutty joined him.

'Look,' he said. 'Look what I done!'

Nutty grinned. It was the first, the very first, inch of achievement, she realised, out of all the hundreds of metres that lay ahead: the look on Hoomey's face. She laughed. Hoomey laughed.

'That was great!'

'Better than I've ever done!'

'You could make it to the end now, and I'll tell old Sam you've done a length.'

'It's fantastic!'

Nutty switched her attention once more to the deep end, where it seemed that Nails was giving Jazz a compulsory lesson in turns. This was as elementary as his lesson to Hoomey: from the side of the bath he put his foot on the back of Jazz's head as he came to the side, and stepped in, taking Jazz's head with him, forcing an abrupt and most accomplished somersault. But Jazz did not seem to appreciate the beautiful simplicity of his achievement, and struck out at Nails under the water. He wore a steel bracelet on his wrist – something to do with being a Sikh, Nutty understood, for it was allowed at school – and caught Nails across the cheekbone. There was a frenzied melee of blood and bubbles, reminding Nutty of a shark drama, fierce blasts of the lifeguard's whistle and an eager slapping of wet feet along the side of the bath as everyone congregated to watch the drama. Nutty sighed heavily, turned away, not wanting to know. Jazz, unlike Hoomey, had backbone, but Nails would not appreciate retaliation. She heard shouts, swearing, cheering, forced herself to look, shut her eyes again. The lifeguard had to go in to part them, cigarette and all, and flung them out like a polo man shooting goal, his large hand projecting them one after the other by the backs of their trunks.

'And you, Nicholson, you show your face in here again for a week and I'll personally hold you under till you drown. Jumping on swimmers is dangerous and absolutely forbidden. You know the rules.'

'I was *teachin'* –'

'I'll teach you a thing or two, my lad! Clear off now, and come back when you can act civil – give us all a break. Off you go, or I'll get the manager!'

Nutty trailed after him to the entrance to the changing rooms.

'Nails – wait –'

He turned his bloody, furious face on her.

'What you want then? That flaming coon with his knuckle-duster –'

'Shut up, Nails. You gave him a fright. He didn't even know it was you. You're a super teacher, but too keen, that's all. Honest, don't get mad! When you're changed, wait for the rest and I'll buy you a coke. And some crisps, if you like. Whatever you want.'

'Huh!' Nails scowled furiously, but would fall for the offer, Nutty knew, being perennially starved and short of cash.

'I'll get the others. Lay off Jazz – he didn't mean it. Chips as well, if you like.'

She wished she could supervise the boys' changing, keep them apart, but it was impossible. She waited for them, duly fed them, smoothed them down. They went outside. It was pouring down with rain, and she had Midnight to ride. She had her own thing to do. She left them, running for her bus, fed up with her responsibilities.

10

Strangely enough, no ill-feeling affected the group of boys she left behind. Their only disenchantment was directed at the weather. They stood on the concrete steps reviewing the dismal scene as if it were a personal insult.

Nails said suddenly, 'Wait here,' and ran off round the corner.

'What's he up to?' Jazz growled.

Gary was grinning.

There was no incentive to move, for the bus queues were twice as long as usual; the rush-hour had started, and the prospect of the long wait in the rain did not appeal. They were standing there, eating crisps, their minds blank, when suddenly a smart green mini pulled up at the steps before them. There was a sharp toot on the horn and the door was thrown open.

'Get in quick!' It was Nails in the driving-seat. The hoarse urgency of his voice galvanized them into action before their minds had taken in what was happening. They were in, piled one on top of the other, and away fast before the significance of the situation fully sank in.

Hoomey thought he was going to faint.

'*Nails*, it's stealing!'

'Borrowin', fathead. You don't want to get wet do you?'

'But the cops –'

'They're all in the dry, drinkin' tea, twit. 'S'no risk at all, this time of day.' He laughed, enjoying their concern. 'Y'ought to be pleased, havin' a taxi. You ought to show a bit of gratitude, the things I do for you.'

He drove fast and cheerfully. It was the first time Hoomey had ever seen him look happy. Nails spun the mini through the traffic, heading out of town, flicking up and down through the gears as if he did it every day. He probably did, Hoomey realised coldly. The others were very quiet, with excited, apprehensive looks on their faces. If they made it, it was going to be great. If not . . . Only Gary was unconcerned, looking out of the window. The rest of them wriggled down in their seats, not wanting to be seen, not daring to say anything.

'You'd better take us up to the refrigerator factory,' Gary said. 'We got to feed those horses.'

'Okay. I'll wait for you.'

'No need to wait,' Bean said awkwardly. 'We all live near. We can walk home after.'

'Gary doesn't, does he? I'll wait for you. If I gotta wait for him, I might as well wait for you too, mightn't I?'

Nobody bothered to argue with Nails. They sat in silence, their pulses thumping, breathing on the windows to encourage the steaming-up process, desperately anxious to get out. Nails turned into the industrial estate roadway, and roared up the hill to the hangar-like stables at the top.

'There you are. You ought to be bloody *pleased*, this weather.'

Their lack of enthusiasm for the venture obviously disgusted him.

They got out, grinning with relief, and pelted into the factory. The rain was hammering on the perspex roof, gurgling in the gutters, and the four horses gazed at them hopefully from over the refrigerator tops, making funny little whickering noises for food. After the alarms of the last hour or so, Hoomey, Bean and Jazz were relieved to turn to the calming chores of mucking out and filling haynets. Nutty had given them a thorough grounding in the process, and put out the evening feeds ready, not trusting them to get the quantities right. Gary added some more oats to his bucket when no one was looking, and stopped to watch his mare eat. Nails came in and stood by him, not saying anything. It was as if something in the skinny mare compelled him; he did not look at any of the others.

Hoomey saw his chance and slipped out into the rain. Bones

was fed and happy, and Hoomey wanted to be the same. He ran all the way home, keeping well off the road in case Nails came in the car and insisted on giving him another lift. He didn't want to be a juvenile delinquent. Who had said he lacked ambition? It was true. He just wanted a quiet, restful life. He was sitting in front of the television, having just that, about an hour later when his mother put her head round the door and said, 'What've you done with your swimming things, love?'

Hoomey thought back, and could not remember having them when he had run home through the rain. He had been unencumbered, panting and slithering over the streaming pavements. He'd left them in the refrigerator factory . . .? No, he couldn't remember putting them down anywhere. And it came to him, with a cold steely horror chilling the bloodstream as if from a lethal injection – he had left them in the stolen mini. He sat, petrified, the implications of his carelessness seeping into his brain. His swimming trunks had a name-tape sewn to the waistband: J. Rossiter. Nails was very unlikely to have left the car in the same place as he had taken it from; he never did, it was too inconvenient. Even now the police might be looking for it, might even have found it, might be fumbling over the wet bundle, opening it out, fingering the name-tape . . .

He leapt to his feet.

'I left them behind!'

'Well, that's careless. But they'll be handed in, I daresay.'

'I'll go and get them!'

'Not now. Don't be daft. Tomorrow'll do.'

'No, truly! I want to go!'

'It's pouring, lovey. It doesn't matter.'

'I must go! It's – it's running – running practice . . . I'm starting tonight. I said I would!'

He leapt towards the front door, scooping his anorak off the hallstand as he went.

'John!'

The cold evening rain blasted him, sweeping up from the sea. It was dark, and the street-lamps cast great wet pools at his feet. The bus had passed him as he left the house; there wasn't another for twenty minutes and no time to wait, only run, heading for Nails's house, praying he would be there. After that, he didn't know what he would do, for Nails would have to decide. Nails would do it. Nails would have to do it, for his own skin as well as his, Hoomey's.

It took him twenty minutes to get down to the town centre and turn into the street of tatty terraced houses behind the bus station where Nails lived. Which house it was he wasn't sure. He had an agonising stitch and his lungs were bursting out of his ribcage, the salt sea-drizzle and the salt sweat mingling in rivers down the side of his nose and into his gasping mouth. He staggered to a halt, peering at the houses. There was an old lorry parked at the end, loaded with scaffolding poles. He tried the house opposite, and was told two doors down. Two doors down had grimy windows and grimier curtains, and a light shining from the kitchen. Hoomey knocked.

Nails came to the door, looking dubious and unwelcoming.

'I – I left – I left my – oh, Jeez, Nails, where'd you leave – that car?'

'I left it behind the Odean. What's up?'

'I – I left my swimming things – in it.'

'Oh, Gawd.'

Nails contemplated the wrecked Hoomey, clutching at his stitch, aware immediately of the dangers of the situation.

'You got your name in 'em then?'

'Yes.'

Nails jerked his head to indicate that Hoomey should come in, as Stalin was yelling from the back, 'Shut the bloody door or do you want us all blown up the chimney?'

Hoomey stepped inside. Nails shut the door and stood gazing into space, silent, apparently thinking. The room had lino on the floor and a plastic three-piece suite gathered round a chipped tile fireplace all covered in dust, but through the door into the kitchen Hoomey could see a more homely scene, with Stalin and Gary watching football on a television set that sat on top of a refrigerator beside the sink. Stalin sat at the table, drinking a can of beer.

57

Nails said, towards the kitchen door, 'I'm goin' out,' picked up a leather jacket that lay on the floor, shrugged it on and opened the door again.

'We'd better get 'em. You are a –' He reeled off a choice string of unpleasant epithets, but without rancour. Like a trueborn criminal he seemed able to take such setbacks in his stride. Hoomey followed him with a feeling of profound respect, even admiration, his panic soothed, his responsibilities comfortably shifted. His heart was still banging away unhealthily and his breath was wheezing with its late efforts, but he knew things were under control again. They slapped their way hastily along the wet pavements, into the main road, up one block and down the side-road that flanked the cinema. There were not many people about and the cinema park was lined with a meagre row or two of takers. The green Mini stood bare and unashamed on its own, in the middle.

Nails paused in the gateway, regarding the scene.

'It's unlocked. Go and get 'em.'

He came too, sauntering, but his eyes on the lookout.

'Other side.'

He pushed Hoomey round to the far door, opened it. Hoomey pushed the front seat up and leaned over, groping about on the back seat. His fingers closed on the soggy bundle. At the same time he felt Nails's hand descend on the back of his neck, pushing him down.

'Bloody hell! Keep down! It's the fuzz!'

Keeping bent double, Hoomey wriggled in a frenzy back out of the door.

'What d'you mean –?'

'Bloody police car! Get down! Jeez!'

Even the redoubtable Nails was panicking now. He dropped on his stomach and wriggled underneath the Mini. Hoomey followed him, spurred by a great slashing of headlights on the wet tarmac and the swish of approaching tyres. He rolled over, banged his head, dragged his stupid swimming things after him, choked with fright. This was quite beyond his worse imaginings. The black haven beneath the car was so small that he had to press

58

himself hard against Nails.

The police car stopped close beside the mini and two pairs of feet shod in heavy black leather appeared close beside Hoomey's bulging eyes. They separated and one pair walked round to the driving side. The car door was opened. Mutterings and gropings from above . . . Hoomey could hear nothing specific above the diesel thumping noise of his own heart . . . some sort of bad-tempered conversation. The engine of the police car was still running. They did not intend to stay long. The other pair of feet moved round to join the pair by the driver's door . . . long pause. The Mini bounced as its door was slammed shut. The feet moved away out of sight. Hoomey could see Nails's eyeballs pale and gleaming in the darkness. The rain pattered down softly and dripped off the Mini's rusty edges, trickling to join the puddle they were already lying in. The few moments seemed like eternity: no movement, no conversation, no development.

Then, without warning, car doors slammed and the police car drove off.

Hoomey and Nails heard its engine recede into the distance. They relaxed, sagging apart, but lay without moving for some time after the car had departed. Hoomey was so relieved he felt like bursting into tears, but with Nails beside him he forced himself to affect nonchalance.

'That was close,' Nails said briefly.

He rolled out cautiously. Hoomey followed. The car park was deserted.

'The owner must've reported it missing. We'd better disappear before he comes to collect,' Nails said.

Hoomey thought Nails would make for home, the mission accomplished, but he seemed disposed to come in Hoomey's direction.

'You going home now?' he asked.

'Yeah. My ma'll be mad at me.' Hoomey still felt shattered, weaker at the knees than usual. 'Thanks, Nails,' he added, embarrassed. 'I was in a sweat.'

'I'll come as far as Tucker's, get some fags,' Nails said.

Tucker's was a corner shop on Hoomey's way home. Hoomey

was not anxious for Nails to accompany him, but Nails fell in beside him, slouching along with his hands in his pockets, his face sullen. Hoomey felt a compulsion to babble on about what had happened, stimulated by their dice with the law, but Nails, now it was over, seemed unmoved. He was silent, scowling, and Hoomey was too uncertain of him to say anything.

When they got to the shop Hoomey, relieved, said goodbye.

'And thanks, Nails. It would've been awful if they'd found my things in the car.'

Nails did not go into the shop but stood looking up the road.

'You going home then?'

'Yes.'

'You don't go back to the horses again?'

'Not after they're fed, no.'

Nails looked down at his feet, soaked in frayed plimsolls. It struck Hoomey then that Nails did not want to go home, even – possibly – that he wanted company. Why else had he come up to Tucker's for fags when he could have got them closer to home? Nails was always roaming about on his own but on a night like this there was not much attraction in it. Hoomey, for a moment or two, was tempted to say, 'Come back with me and we'll watch the soccer replay on the box,' but he did not think his mother would approve of Nails – not if she *knew*. But, looking at him now, he seemed harmless enough. He looked lonely, if the truth were told. Slightly pathetic. But Hoomey knew Nails was not like that.

'Well, I'll be getting home. Thanks, Nails.'

Nails shrugged.

Hoomey set off up the hill, half running, so relieved he could have cried.

Nails stood looking at his feet for some time, as there was not much else to do. He thought of Hoomey's house a few hundred yards up, his stooge of a VATman dad smoking his pipe in front of the fire and his fat mum in the kitchen . . . Nails knew them both by sight; they would'nt say boo to a goose, called each other mum and dad, even when they were alone together, homely sorts. Nails' mum and dad had never been homely sorts. They had quarrelled all the time and his mum had slammed out and left all the washing-up in the sink which he and Gary had to do when they ran out of plates. It was more peaceful now she was gone for good, but miserable. No meals, no fires, no welcome. After he had slept in the same sheets for six months Nails had taken them to the launderette, and now he had discovered a few things like that, which helped, which is more than his dad ever had. Nails did not like evenings at home, which is why he stayed out. But staying out at night cost money if you did the right things: coffee bars and a movie or a disco, but if you rode round in borrowed cars it was an okay way of killing time. But now, after his near miss with Hoomey, Nails remembered that he was for the long drop next time – no more cautions. He'd run out of cautions. Next time it was a detention centre.

Nails sighed heavily. If he'd had a nice meal by the fire and the box to watch and no screaming and yelling he'd have stayed in like Hoomey. He supposed you got bored with too much of it, but just at the moment it seemed very desirable. He had thought for a moment that Hoomey was going to ask him back, but he knew he wasn't the sort of friend that nice mothers were all that pleased to see. He wasn't insensitive and could read such atmospheres without much difficulty.

Now he was so close he thought he might call on Gary's horse before he went home. He had liked it terrifically when he had seen it before but hadn't wanted to say: it seemed girlish to him to think anything of an animal. But there was no one to see him now. Hoomey had said no one would go back there tonight and it was as good a place to mooch about in as any other.

He went across the waste ground, not bothering to avoid the puddles any more, his feet slopping. There was not a soul to be seen, which was hardly surprising, considering. It was no night to be out in if one had a choice. That was the nice thing about the horses' strange stable: its cathedral-like aloofness from the weather. Once inside, it was a world of its own, the heavy doors pulled to, a sense of tranquillity pervading the echoing space. The horses were eating their hay. The rhythmic, monotonous noise of their chewing was soothing to Nails. The horses turned their heads to look at him, but were not disturbed, except the mare which had been allocated to Gary. She stopped in mid bite and her ears went back warily. Nails went up to her. Now he was alone he did not mind committing himself.

'What's the matter, beautiful?'

The mare moved restlessly round her box, not taking her eyes off him. Nails was fascinated by her nervous movement. He climbed over the refrigerators and dropped into the straw beside her. She backed away quickly and stood as far from him as she could, cringing like a dog, her tail clamped down hard, her nostrils dilated with fear.

'Why are you frightened?'

Like him, lying underneath that mini . . . his heart had been going overtime then, thinking of the law closing down on him.

'You haven't got anything to be frightened of – not here . . . Best of everything you're getting, like a blooming racehorse. Not like when you were on the way to the knacker's – that was different, wasn't it?'

Except that she wouldn't have known, not until she got there and smelled the blood. Nails, without thinking, sat down in the comfortable straw and talked to the mare, leaning his head against the refrigerator wall. He felt an affinity with the horse; she was a drop-out horse, one of the great rejected, like him. But luck had come her way at the very last moment. It was the same, animals and humans, if you struck lucky . . . you could be an Olympic show-jumper or Seb Coe, adored by millions, or you could be knacker-meat, horse or human. He wasn't far off knacker-meat himself. An unaccustomed self-pity overtook him, sitting in the straw, and he went into a trance, thinking of all the ways he lost out, trying to think of one positive factor in his favour. The only thing he could think of was he was a good swimmer – and a fat lot of good that was to him. He'd rather have had warm feet at that moment.

Lying under that police car just now, he knew he had gone down about as far as he could go, had expected to be caught, done for. Nobody would have cared; been relieved, more like, to have him out of the way. He had got bored with driving around in cars anyway. He really was fed up, come to think of it. Even this lark of Gary's was something, having a horse and learning to shoot straight. If it had gone with his image, Nails thought he could have been quite interested. He would like to do it, in fact, but not with old Sylvester and Foggerty and all cheering him on. He thought he could jolly well do it better than Hoomey and co: he could swim and run, at least, which was halfway there, and he bet he could learn riding quicker than them. If old Deirdre MacTavish could do it, anyone could, surely? He thought of himself, stunning them all by running and swimming and riding and shooting better than the lot of them, and them all eating their words and cheering and him being cool, man.

While he was fantasizing in this way the mare seemed to get used to his being there and when he next took notice of her she was quite close to him and looking at him curiously, head stretched out, upper lip quivering. When he moved she jumped back like a startled rabbit.

He was intrigued, and sat still until she approached again and then, very gently, he put a hand out towards her. She put back her ears but did not move. In a minute or two she licked his hand with a wet, rough tongue. He was a bit frightened, thinking she would bite, but stayed without moving so that she wouldn't jump back again. She took a step nearer, and her ears moved into the forward position. Nails felt touched, that she liked him. He wondered if she liked Gary.

'You'd be better off with me,' he said. 'I'd like you better than Gary.'

It occurred to him that if she belonged to Gary, there was nothing to stop him taking a sort of family ownership too. If he told Gary, Gary was bound to agree. It would be *their* horse, and he could learn to ride it – in the evenings perhaps, when there was nobody about. He liked this idea.

'You like me, don't you?'

The mare was indicating that she did, standing companionably in the darkening stable, lipping at his anorak sleeve. Nails laid

back and made himself comfortable. He told himself she understood him because, like him, she was knackermeat, really – but
she had come lucky. She ought to be called Lucky. Lucky
Something, a double-barrelled name like a smart horse, not just
ordinary Lucky like an old mongrel. He lay thinking of smart
names. The other horses clonked and snorted softly in the
darkness behind their partitions, so that he did not feel at all
alone, but in a sort of family. It was warm and odourous in a nice
family way. He liked it. He remembered old dad VATman up at
Hoomey's sitting by the fire and how he had wanted to go there,
and that made him think of a good name: Lucky Fireside . . . no,
Firelight, Lucky Firelight. It fitted, because she was chestnut like
Firelight. She had a little white star on her face. Lucky *Lady*
Firelight . . . that made it better – that was smart all right! He felt
quite excited at the thought of such a good name. Much too good
for Gary, he thought.

He would have to think about what he could do to get to ride
her. But without them all knowing.

II

Miss Bedwelty lived some ten miles away in 'proper country'
(signs of habitation at infrequent intervals). Five passengers – as
Nutty insisted on coming – could hardly squeeze into Mr Sylvester's car, so he arranged to borrow the school minibus. Any sense
of importance this might have invoked was quelled by pure funk
– in Hoomey's case, at least – of what lay ahead. Even Jazz was
not very optimistic.

'It's a girl's thing, riding,' he said.

'So, Harvey Smith's a poofter?' Nutty grated at him. 'And
Lester Piggott and –'

'We're not – we're not *them* –' Why did she have to use such
pinnacles of perfection to lure them with?

Nutty was in a bad temper because Nails wanted to come too. First she said there was no room in the car, but when Mr Sylvester said he would use the minibus her excuse was jerked from under her feet.

'That's OK then,' Nails said. 'I can come.'

'Who said? You're swimming, not riding.'

'I'm a trainer, aren't I? I'm part of the team if I'm a trainer. I do more than you. I've got a right.'

Nutty could not think of a good answer and nor could Mr Sylvester, so Nails was allowed to come. They were surprised by his zeal and suspected trouble, but Nails was amenable and even civil during the journey, mystifying them still further. But the evening was too fraught to bother about Nails. Of all the skills, riding was the ultimate test and the one the team viewed with the least enthusiasm. Mucking out and feeding the beasts, although a chore, was nothing compared to actually getting on top of them, entrusting one's breakable frame to such unreliable support. Hoomey was more frightened of doing it than anything else, even the swimming, and yet, curiously, it was the one thing he actually *wanted* to succeed at. He wanted to succeed because he did not want to let poor old Bones down. He really did want to ride Bones, not just groom him and feed him carrots. He had a beautiful dream of riding Bones like you saw people on the television, leaping great fences, seen from low down so that they looked about ten feet high. He did not think he could ever be that kind of a person but Nutty said some of the best riders were the quiet, sympathetic ones. She had not exactly said 'wet' and 'weedy', but 'quiet' and 'sympathetic', and Hoomey supposed that showed her tact, because he thought that was what she meant.

He had something else on his mind too, but was not allowed to divulge it to anybody else, under the threat of being 'pulped to mush'. The morning after he had left his swimming things in the stolen Mini, when he had gone up early to see old Bones, he had found Nails fast asleep in the straw in the chestnut mare's box. He had arrived before the others, and got the shock of his life when he saw Nails. Nails had woken up abruptly and been angry

65

at being discovered, and had gone out into the grey morning without any conversation beyond the threat about pulping Hoomey if he split. Hoomey had not seen Nails there since, but had an instinct that he had come the following night too. The nervous little mare had seemed unaccountably quieter, and the straw was flattened in the corner. Hoomey thought it very weird, and longed to discuss it with somebody, but daren't, not even to ask Gary if Nails had been away at night. Hoomey was afraid Nails was up to mischief. He could think of no harmless reason for Nails's strange trespass. He could think of no reason for it at all, in fact. Whenever he looked thoughtfully at Nails, Nails glowered back in a thoroughly unfriendly manner.

Miss Bedwelty's place was a slightly shabby but tidy yard laid round a gravelled square, with a large indoor school – looking not unlike the refrigerator warehouse – looming behind. The place seemed to be swarming with little horsey girls who vied to do Miss Bedwelty's bidding.

'Tack up Red Flag, Seashell, Parky and Joe and bring them into the school,' she ordered, and the little girls fled away, while Miss Bedwelty gave her new pupils another of her withering stares.

'See what you're made of,' she promised.

They went into the school as the girls brought out the ponies, a docile, shiny lot compared with the animals at home, Hoomey decided. The one he was allocated, Parky, a homely, Hoomey-sized bay, was a piece of cake compared with Bones. Hoomey, accustomed to avoiding Bones's enormous feet and keeping his hands away from the ever-questing lips, like two grey motor-tyres devouring anything remotely edible, was enchanted with Parky's dainty obedience. His confidence increased as a friendly girl came to show him how to mount. It was easy on Parky, not requiring a step-ladder, and not nearly so far to fall once aboard. The whole business here at Miss Bedwelty's seemed far less daunting than it did out on the industrial estate. Perhaps this riding lark was a lot better than he had been anticipating.

But Nutty, slouched against the wall watching with Nails and Mr Sylvester, felt a great gloom settle as the full responsibility of her captaincy overcame her. They had about six months in which to achieve their miracle, she and Nails and Mr Sylvester, and the riding was her department, a hurdle of the most gigantic proportions. Six months to get Hoomey jumping Bones . . . watching him, Nutty saw the very rawest of raw beginners, sitting pop-eyed with excitement on a pony quiet enough to put your great-grandmother on. He lurched at every step and emitted squeaks of either joy or horror – it was impossible to tell – when the pony trotted a couple of paces to catch up with its companions. Hoomey, Nutty would have said, had no natural talent. The same applied to her cousin Bean but Jazz, if he had never ridden before, had a natural balance that made him look positively accomplished beside the other two. Gary was bolder than Hoomey, less graceful than Jazz, but showed the Nicholson family characteristics of dour determination to win through against all the odds. Of the four, Nutty saw hope for two – given twice their allocated time and decent, trained horses to ride.

Miss Bedwelty, having asked Sam what their horse situation was, was saying, 'I take it yours are all schoolmasters, suitable for what you're asking?'

Sam, who did not know the term schoolmaster was ever applied to the equine, looked puzzled.

'They're horses.'

'Horses that can teach your youngsters what to do? Horses are like humans in many respects, you know – some you can trust your children with and some you can't. I think I'd better come over and see what material you are intending to work with.'

Nutty guessed that some instinct told Sam to keep his mouth shut about the knacker-yard history.

'They're a – er – a mixed bag, what the PA could afford.'

'Huh,' said Miss Bedwelty, with a wealth of feeling. 'Good horses never come cheap.'

Sam maintained a tactful silence.

On the way home Hoomey and Jazz declared themselves much in favour of riding, Gary was non-committal and Bean said it was horrible. Nails was silent and scowling. Miss Bedwelty had said she would come over to see their horses the following week.

'She won't think anything of 'em, sir,' Nutty said earnestly when they were driving home.

'What's wrong with them? Apart from needing fattening up?'

Nutty could not begin to say, amongst the so obvious short-comings: too big, too old, too nervous, too dull, too run-down, too absolutely bloody hopeless, like the team itself. She sighed deeply. Sam did not pursue the subject. Driving back into town, he put them down near their homes, Nutty, Nails and Gary getting out last down by the bus-station. After he had driven away, Nails turned to Nutty and said, 'Can I come up to yours? I want to talk to you.'

'If you want.' Nutty was surprised and not too keen.

Gary started to walk with them but Nails told him to clear off home. 'It's just trainers,' he said. 'Private.'

Gary went.

Nutty said, to put Nails off, 'I've got to ride now. I haven't time to talk. It'll be dark soon.'

'Yeah, okay, I'm not stopping you. I just want to ask you something.'

'What?'

'This riding thing – will you teach me?'

Nutty stopped in her tracks. Nails was looking his most belligerent, and spoke almost angrily.

'*Me* teach you?'

'I'd pay you.'

'Why not join in with the others, if you want to learn?'

'I – I – no, it's a secret,' he mumbled. 'And Sam wouldn't let me.'

Nutty was silent, amazed.

Nails said defiantly, 'There ought to be a reserve in this team, in case. All teams have a reserve.'

'Well, ask Sam.'

'They wouldn't let me do anything,' Nails said aggressively, and with a fair amount of truth. 'S'no good asking *them*. I don't want favours. I'd pay you. It was your idea for me to do the swimming, so I thought you could do the same for me.'

'It's not the same.'

'Why not? Besides, it's business – I said I'd pay you. Whatever the cost is . . . what people charge.'

'Proper people charge about three quid an hour.' As she said it Nutty thought, three quid for an hour's work. She looked with more interest at Nails.

'You got a pony,' Nails said. 'You could show me somewhere. The others needn't know.'

'When would we do it?'

'After swimming? I could meet you somewhere where you could show me. An' I'd pay you three pounds.'

'Where'd you get the money from?'

'My dad, he gives me money.'

That was news to Nutty, as Nails was perennially skint and starving.

'Well, if it's a job, like –' Nutty worked it out carefully. 'Once a week perhaps. We could go up on the railway sidings.'

They had pulled the rails up and there was an expanse of cindery ground suitable for a school. 'Nobody goes there now, only in the summer – a few motor-bikes. Nobody would see.'

'I don't want anybody to know. You're not to say to anyone, or I'll kill you.'

'No.' Nutty knew she wouldn't, not being too sure about taking the money. But the money was a great temptation.

'Will you?'

'We could try it.'

'When, tonight?'

'Hey, give me a chance!'

'Why not?'

'No. You got to meet me up the railway. Say – um – Friday.'

'Okay. Friday.'

'Six o'clock.'

Nails turned and disappeared the way they had come, leaving Nutty much intrigued. There was no one to discuss this strange development with and, as she saddled and bridled the eager Midnight for their ride, Nutty could not help feeling astonished by Nails's request. What ulterior motive lay behind his desire to ride? Perhaps he did want to be in the team? If only he could be! If she could be too – then they might stand a chance against those racy Greycoat boys! At least Nails was not afraid of suffering a bit; he had come by his name because he was so hard. And Jazz . . . Jazz was okay and Gary might do, but Bean and *Hoomey*! God help them! The vision of Miss Bedwelty inspecting Hoomey on Bones was blanch-making. Gasworks Olympic contenders . . . oh, Jeez, Nutty thought: something would just have to turn up, or else the whole thing was a dead duck.

12

If Nutty had known how Nails intended to get the money for her fees she would have been shocked. Nutty was right about Nails having no money. But Nails did not consider his lack an impediment to his plans. If one wanted money enough one went out and acquired it – it was like cars in this respect. On Thursday night – late night shopping – Nails went down to the supermarket in his anorak with the big pockets and lifted six electric plugs, four pairs of scissors and a pair of pillowcases which he sold to a friend of his father's for three pounds. He felt more uneasy about this than about borrowing cars, but considered that the reason he wanted the money for was worthy: not as if it was coke or ciggies or similar self-indulgence. It was for self improvement, if you like. With the money safely in his pocket, he felt a strange and most unfamiliar feeling of pleased anticipation stirring inside him; he was really looking forward to his appointment with Nutty, to find out what it felt like to ride a horse. He kept thinking of Lucky Lady Firelight and himself aboard, constraining that nervous power that so intrigued him. He thought if Nutty just showed him, once or twice – just the basics – he would be able to ride his mare when no one was around, at night. He would have to find out how the bridle went on, and things like that. But not enough to make old Deirdre suspicious. She was sharp for a girl. You didn't think of her as a girl somehow.

He had got bored with cars and the business with Lucky Lady Firelight seemed more challenging. The prospect of Sam's motorbike, mouth-watering as it was, was too far off coming true to be worth thinking about yet, if ever. Getting Hoomey to swim ten lengths was . . . well, you'd need to be a magician, Nails thought, not a teacher.

On Friday at school he passed Nutty in the corridor and gave her a fierce stare to remind her about their appointment and she said, 'I haven't forgotten,' in an aggrieved voice. It was a cold lousy day and drizzling by evening. Nails got up to the railway sidings early. They covered a large tract of ground, quite deserted, but conveniently illuminated by the high powerful lights round the warehouses that separated it from the still-working mainline railway. The electric commuter trains rattled past at frequent intervals while Nails mooched impatiently up and down, kicking an old tin can and wishing he didn't have to be dependent on a girl. Not on anybody. He liked to work alone.

Nutty arrived on time, thudding out of the dusk and pulling to an abrupt halt. Nails, now a connoisseur of horses, looked critically at Midnight and saw that he possessed the same nervous temperament as Lucky Lady Firelight, and was pleased. He was not attracted to dull horses.

Nutty did not waste time. She dismounted, took off her hat and thrust it at Nails.

'I don't want a hat.'

'You've got to. Else no lesson.'

Nails put it on.

'Put your left foot in the stirrup, facing like this. And don't prod him with your toe. He doesn't like it. Don't pull on the back of the saddle. And don't land heavily, he doesn't like that either.'

Nails, being agile, mounted without difficulty. Nutty showed him how to hold the reins. There were two, but she knotted one up out of the way. She then attached a long lungeing rein which she had brought coiled over her shoulder to Midnight's noseband.

71

'What's that? I don't want to be led.'

'You've got to. He'll belt off with you if I don't. He's not a learner's pony. He's a JA show-jumper and he's valuable. If he belts off he might hurt himself.'

It wasn't easy to argue with Nutty. She led Midnight to a clear patch and then let him walk on the long rein, so that she stayed still and he walked round her in a circle at the end of the rein. At least he was supposed to walk, but he kept trotting. Nails gritted his teeth and willed himself to stay squarely in the saddle.

'Keep your hands down. Don't pull on his mouth. Hands down, shorten your reins. Lean forward more, and put your lower leg back, let your knees bend and your feet go back, heels down.'

Midnight jiggled and cavorted and let out two enormous bucks. Nails flew through the air and landed heavily on the cindery ground, grazing his hands and his cheek. He got up and went back to the pony, climbing on as Nutty had told him. He was furiously angry.

'Shorten your reins. He's got to get his head down to buck, so be ready for him.'

Nutty did not seem to care, concerned only for the pony.

'Don't pull on his mouth. Just be ready if he ducks his head, to hold it up. But if you keep pulling on the reins he'll get cross.'

Shorten your reins . . . don't pull . . . Nails bit his tongue as Midnight jiggled and swung about on the end of the rein. Nutty shouted imperiously at the pony, and then encouraged him in a sing-song voice, 'Trot on, trot on, one two, one two.'

The pony started to trot more steadily. Nails was thrown about, feeling like a sack of potatoes, jerked in all directions, but Nutty had no mercy, keeping the pony going.

After a bit she shouted, 'The trot has a one-two rhythm. If you rise up in the stirrups when I say one and sink down at two you'll find you stay with it.'

Just occasionally Nails managed it, and saw that finding the rhythm and rising and falling to it was the nub of the whole uncomfortable business, but it did not happen very often. Nutty

72

stopped Midnight and brought him into the centre and Nails thought he was going to get a rest, but she immediately sent him off in the other direction.

'Bad for him to do it only one way,' she said.

Nails thought it was bad for him which ever way.

'*One* two, *one* two,' Nutty intoned.

Nails concentrated hard and found the stride about once in every two circles, but could not keep with it for more than two or three strides before he lost his balance and came down while Midnight was coming up.

It felt to him like an hour before Nutty stopped Midnight again. She came up to him.

'How does it feel?'

Nails shrugged.

'Bloody awful.'

'You're not bad. A few more times and you'd get it. D'you want to canter?'

He shrugged again. It was awful making such a fool of himself in front of Nutty.

'It's easier,' Nutty said. 'Just sit still, and let yourself go with it. Hold the front of the saddle if you like. Don't hold on by the reins whatever you do.'

She sent Midnight to the end of the rein and got him trotting. Nails bit his tongue and slithered all over the place.

'Can – ter! Can – ter!' Nutty called out sharply.

There was a slight lurch and suddenly Nails found that all was sweetness and light; he was moving with delicious ease, his bottom glued to the saddle, no slithering, no jerking, no bumping, just a pleasant sensation of moving to a smooth, easy rhythm. It was a revelation after the pain of trotting and Nails was cross when Nutty brought it to an end. Midnight came to a halt, snorting and pawing the ground. Nutty came up and patted his neck.

'That's enough for the first time.'

'That was nice.'

'Oh, yes, he's got a beautiful canter. Nothing to it.'

If it hadn't been for the canter Nails would not have been

73

terribly keen for another lesson, but the canter had given him dreams above his station.

'What are you doing it for?' Nutty asked him.

'I'm paying you, aren't I?' he countered angrily.

He thrust the money at her.

'You ought to be in the team,' she said. 'You're better than all of them.'

'What would I want to be in a stupid team for?' He pulled off the hat and thrust it back at her. 'Bein' told what to do all the time? Who wants that?'

'It's better than nobody wanting you.'

Nutty put her hat back on and coiled up her lungeing rein. Nails was already on his way, turning his back and heading for the railway line. Nutty mounted and rode after him.

'Do you want another lesson? Next week?'

'I don't care.'

'Nor do I particularly.'

'Well then.'

Nails climbed through the fence on to the railway line.

'Get lost,' he said.

'Thank *you*,' said Nutty. She turned Midnight on his hocks and went away at a canter. Nails watched her, wild feelings of frustration rising up in a familiar cauldron in his breast. 'Nobody wanting you . . .' The words flooded him with self-pity. He started to kick the fence until it hurt, the tears running down his face, safely alone amongst the sidings.

13

Angry with Nutty for her pigheadedness and superior airs, Nails did not turn up for the next swimming lesson. Nutty, furious, attacked him bitterly in school the next morning.

'Some trainer you are, just not bothering!'

74

'I never promised, did I? Nobody wants me in the team, only to do the sweating, making Hoomey an' all swim. They all know it's hopeless, that's why they asked me.'

'Since when did you want to be in the team? It's news to me!'

'I never said I did –'

'Sounds like you want it to me. Excuse me if I misread you.'

Nails had a job to stop swiping Nutty one.

'It doesn't come into it! I'm just telling you, what they want me for –'

'It was my idea asking you. Now you've let me down they'll just say, we told you so, Sam and Foggerty and all. I gave you a riding lesson, didn't I? I didn't let *you* down.'

'Yeah, but I bet you won't give me another.'

'Who said? You said you didn't care.'

Nails kicked the wall, hating the way she turned his words on him.

'Do you want?' she insisted.

He shrugged. He wanted desperately, but he wasn't having her know that.

'I don't care.'

Nutty stared hard at him. Then she said, quite good-temperedly, 'Why don't you come up tonight when Miss Bed-welty comes to see the horses?'

'Why?'

'Why not? You came to hers before. Nobody'll say.'

Nails shrugged. 'I might then.'

'She's coming straight after school while it's still light.'

Nails scuffled off, scowling. Nutty watched him go, puzzled. She could not fathom his belligerence. She would have said he was much attracted by the riding, yet he made out he wasn't. She really wanted him to teach the swimming, believing that they might *achieve* for Nails, even if only because they were frightened not to; that was the reason she had made herself be nice to him, inviting him to come up when Miss Bedwelty came.

She was not prepared for, although not surprised by, Miss Bedwelty's forthright reaction when she saw the animals in the refrigerator factory. Sam took Nutty and her team up in the car

75

straight after the last lesson; Nails had not been around which was just as well as the car did not hold more than five. Miss Bedwelty arrived a few minutes after they did and they all piled into the factory.

'Some stable!' Miss Bedwelty exclaimed, not without a measure of appreciation. 'There's a lot to be said for the barn method. The Aga Khan's new stud at Chantilly is after this new style, I understand.'

Nutty liked the comparison and grinned as Sam said, 'Really? That's great.'

Sam did not know the Aga Khan's stud at Chantilly from a Leyland double decker bus factory in Preston, but he knew how to say the right things. He put the light on, and the four inmates at the far end set up their whickering and pawing at the prospect of food, as usual.

'Let's have 'em out then. I want to see them move. Paces are everything.'

The four horses, amazed by the proceedings, were led into the great outdoors which they surveyed with apathy, fear, suspicion and greed respectively, Bones tugging Hoomey irretrievably to the nearest succulent patch of weed.

'Manners! Manners!' Miss Bedwelty cried out, and as Hoomey's tugging proved ineffectual she crossed over and gave Bones a severe slap across the muzzle, raising his head to receive an aggrieved stare.

'Speak to him firmly. Horses understand whether you mean it or not.'

Even Bones understood Miss Bedwelty. He followed Hoomey unprotestingly back to the others.

Miss Bedwelty stood staring at the horses for some time, standing with her hand on her hips. She made them walk backwards and forwards, and then trot. Then she said, 'Oh, my Gawd,' in a sad voice.

'You must be mad, Mr Sylvester, to think —' she said, 'to think — great deeds can be done — with horses like these.'

Sam looked stunned.

'Not great deeds. Only . . .' He hesitated.

'Mr Sylvester, with these horses and those riders, anything that gets done at all will be a great deed.'

Nutty felt herself flinching at the dreadful truth put into such forthright speech.

'The only way you will get any results at all, is for me to take your boys in my school, on my horses, two or three times a week, from now through until the summer, and for the boys to use my horses for the competition. That will cost you something in the region of fifty pounds a week.'

Sam flinched this time, visibly.

'And what about our horses?'

'Send 'em back where they came from. They're useless.'

'But they came from the knacker's,' Hoomey said.

Miss Bedwelty laughed. 'I might have known!'

There was a long, fraught silence.

Miss Bedwelty then said, 'You asked me up here to give my opinion. It's no good my beating about the bush.'

'You're quite right,' Sam said. 'We'll put them away then.'

He gave Hoomey a little shove on the shoulder. 'On your way, lad. Looks like you're delivered.'

What did he mean, Hoomey wondered? Bones lifted his head and gave Hoomey an affectionate nudge, which nearly knocked him off his feet. Hoomey knew it was a suggestion for sugar-lumps, which he kept in his pocket. When he got two out on the flat of his hand as Nutty had shown him, Bones's great motor-tyre lips closed over them, the rough skin scratching the ticklish palm. Two weeks ago Hoomey knew that he would have been terrified putting any part of his anatomy within an inch of Bones's long, grooved teeth, but habit had given him confidence. There was no malice in Bones, only infinite good nature, a clumsy hope to please, a passing affection for the hand that fed him. His rejection by Miss Bedwelty was unkind. Hoomey felt indignant on Bones's behalf.

'What's she know about you?' he muttered as he led Bones back inside.

14

Two or three days after Miss Bedwelty's visit the team found that nobody pressed them to practise anything, nothing was said about another riding lesson and life was refreshingly peaceful. Only Nutty was worried by this.

On the fourth day she accosted Sam.

'Has anything been decided, sir – about riding lessons?'

'It's been put to the Parents' Association, Deirdre. They're going to give their verdict tonight, as to whether they can afford to pay fifty pounds a week. The feeling is, I think, that it's a lot to spend on only four boys. Disproportionate, you understand. Fifty pounds a week could benefit the whole school, if it were put to other uses.'

'But if they don't, sir, the whole project will be washed up.'

'Well, Deirdre, it could come to that. We seem to have made no progress at all. Not only the riding, but the swimming . . . Your idea about Nails – first he was barred from the pool for a week, then after that you said he never turned up. Mr Foggerty says he can't devote sufficient time to it, so we've made no progress there. I must say my earlier enthusiasm has considerably cooled.'

Nutty was shocked.

'You couldn't back out now, sir. Not now you've said.'

'It could be forced on us. The horse thing is crucial. We can't do it without the support of the PA, you know that.'

'Well, you tell 'em, sir. You tell 'em they've got to.'

But it seemed that the Parents' Association thought fifty pounds a week for merely one phase of the competition excessive. Reports on progress were not encouraging; Sam had to admit in public that the swimming difficulties were also somewhat fearsome: professional coaching in that sphere would also be costly and unprofessional coaching 'posed certain difficulties'.

'You mean the boys are not up to it?'

'I wouldn't say that. More a matter of the amount of time required . . . excessive . . . good coaching does not come cheap . . .'

When the boys heard that Sam's amazing brainchild was to be flushed down the pan they were shattered. The responsibility had lain so heavily that it took some time to readjust. Bean was jubilant, Gary pleased, Jazz silent and non-committal. Hoomey felt as if a large black stormcloud had rolled off him. He could smoke ciggies again and not run up the hill from Tuckers every day to improve his weakly lung-power. He need not undergo terrorist treatment in the swimming bath, not get up at six o'clock every morning to feed old Bones. Life was suddenly full of wide, sunny horizons, blue sky all round.

'You've got to go on doing the horses, idiot, until they go. You can't just leave them!'

Nutty was apoplectic with rage at the decision, and not inclined to hide it.

'Where are they going then?'

'My uncle's taking them back.'

'Back where?'

'Where they were going before, of course.'

'You mean –' Hoomey looked at Nutty with an unexpected lurch of alarm. 'You don't mean – not back to the knacker's?'

'Well – I don't know what he'll do with them, do I? I'm not a mind reader, am I?'

Nutty did know, but Hoomey's expression put her off.

'Honestly, Nutty, tell me, not back to the knacker's?'

'Well, it's likely, isn't it? That's what he bought them for in the first place.'

'He can't!' Hoomey burst out. 'Not Bones! He can't do that now!'

Hoomey had not forseen the consequences of the new decision. The blue skies clouded over abruptly.

'If it means that, I'd rather do all that running an' swimming and stuff! He can't do that to us now – not say we're doing it and then say we're not, and killing old Bones! Hey, Nutty, you're the

79

captain – you can say something, can't you? And what'll Nails say?'

'Why should Nails say anything?'

'About Lucky Lady Firelight.'

'He won't care. Why should he?'

'But he – he –'

Hoomey remembered that Nails would kill him if he told, and hesitated. But everything was different now. Lucky Lady Firelight wasn't lucky any more. She was going back to the knacker's.

'He – Nails – he – he sleeps in her stable every night.'

'You're joking!'

'No. He keeps a sleeping bag up there, stuffed behind the old ventilator pipes, and he sleeps in with her. But you mustn't let on you know – he said he'd kill me. I only told you so you know he – he – well, he *likes* her. Like I like Bones. He won't want her to go to the knacker's either, I bet.'

Hoomey saw an ally in Nails, to help him stop them from sending the horses back to the knacker's. As an ally, Nails was a powerful force.

Nutty was flabbergasted at Hoomey's disclosure. She remembered Nails's dogged determination riding Midnight, swallowing his male arrogance to knuckle under to a girl's instructions: it had really been a struggle for him. He must have wanted it so badly. Why? Was Hoomey's news a clue? Nails wanted to ride Lucky Lady Firelight . . . he had said something about being in the team.

Nutty's eyes were positively glittering.

She said to Hoomey, 'If this team effort is washed up, the horses will have to go, and they'll go back to where they came from, no doubt about that.'

Hoomey looked as if he was going to burst into tears.

'Not Bones!'

'To keep Bones, would you rather go on with the competition?'

Hoomey dithered.

Life did seem rather full of nothing to do since Sam had said the competition was off. He had quite liked the thought of being fit and athletic some time in the future, although the signs had taken a long time coming. He still didn't look any different, but he could run home from Tuckers now without having a seizure on the doorstep.

'Yes,' he said.

Nutty went to Sam.

'Is it really certain – no competition? Have you told the Greycoats lot?'

'No, not yet. But it's certain, yes. The PA won't pay that amount and I don't see we can do it without. And I just don't have the support I had hoped for – from you, perhaps, yes. I'll say that for you, Deirdre, you've been more encouraging than anyone else.'

Deirdre said something like 'Humph!' which made Sam think she would grow up like Miss Bedwelty.

'That's it then?' she said.

'I'm afraid so.'

'When is my uncle taking the horses back?'

'Monday he said.'

Nutty went to look for Nails. He was smoking behind the bicycle sheds.

'I want to talk to you.'

'What's stopping you?'

Nutty sighed.

'Look, it's important. It's about the competition. It seems a shame not to do it just because of what old Bedwelty said.'

'It makes no difference to me.'

'No. I suppose not. And the others don't care either, only Hoomey, because of his Bones having to go to the knacker's.'

'Bones? The horse, you mean?'

'Yes. My uncle's taking them on Monday.'

'All of them?'

'Yes.'

Nutty waited with bated breath, not daring to look at Nails, trying to look bored and world-weary. Nails said nothing. Nutty waited as long as she could.

'I had an idea,' she said slowly. 'To keep the whole thing going. Save the horses from being killed.'

'What's that?' Nails said.

81

Nutty risked looking at him. He had spoken quickly, without thinking, and looked desperately eager for her idea.

'Nobody's said the team's got to be official, like. Just because *they* say it's off, if we want to do it, they can't stop us. And if we make it a decent team – people who are good at – at swimming and riding and all . . .'

She paused. Nails's expression was guarded but still, she would have said, eager underneath.

'If you were in the team, for instance.'

'I can't ride.'

'You're a natural. You'd learn in no time.'

'They wouldn't have me.'

'*They* don't come into it anymore. It's us, our team.'

Nails was silent. Nutty reckoned she was doing well. 'I want to be in the team too,' she said. 'They wouldn't have me because I'm a girl. Well, that's stupid. I can ride the pants off any of those Greycoat boys. And I could learn to swim enough, and run, if I wanted to. More than my cousin Bean and your Gary. They don't *want* to do it. They're useless. But if the team was you and me, for a start, and Jazz is okay – he wants to do it, I can tell the way he looked, and he's bright . . . well, we're halfway there.'

Nails said nothing.

'I'll teach you to ride,' Nutty said. 'You can learn to ride Lucky Lady Firelight, and she wouldn't have to go.'

Nails looked up, pulling fiercely on his stub of home-rolled cigarette. For a moment Nutty was afraid that he knew that Hoomey had given his secret away; but he was not apathetic anymore. His eyes were sharp and interested.

'What good'ld it be,' he asked angrily.

'What good is any bloody thing?' Nutty said, equally angry. 'What's the good driving round in your stupid cars? What good's coming to school, come to that? Whatever we learn – there's no job afterwards.'

Nails scowled.

Nutty said, furious, 'I don't care then! If you don't want, the whole thing's off. I just thought you had a bit more guts than the rest of them. Hoomey's the only one willing, and he's just a weed.

82

But at least he'll try. And you – you're streets ahead of Hoomey –'

'Oh, shut up! I never said I wouldn't. But –'

He was kicking the bicycle rack now, in proper Nailsish fashion, glowering and sparking.

'If you won't it's no go altogether. And the poor nags'll get the chop and Hoomey'll cry. It's a bloody shame!'

'*Shut up*! I never said –'

'No, you never say anything. That's your trouble. Don't commit yourself.'

'You – have you – asked –'

'There's no one to ask. We're on our own.'

'What about the – the money? The horses –'

'My uncle will go on keeping the horses if we want them. I can teach the riding. You can teach the swimming. Running – well, we can all run if we want to. S'only practice. And the shooting – well, if we want to, we can arrange it, I daresay. It's wanting to that matters.'

'We – I suppose – we could see how it goes.'

'You mean you will?'

Nails kicked the bicycle rack so hard that two bikes fell out.

'Well –'

'You're better off than the others, if you take on Gary's horse. It's the best of the lot.'

'I know.'

'I'll talk to Jazz, shall I? Tell him you're interested, just. See what he says. I haven't asked him yet. Hoomey says he will.'

'Hoomey's useless.'

'Yes, but he'll try. He'll do what he's told. You and I can get him moving.'

'Try Jazz then.' Nails pulled furiously on the last of his cigarette, threw it down and stamped on it.

'I'll find him now, let you know.'

Nails nodded and stalked away, head down, hands in pockets.

What a weirdo! Nutty thought. All that pent-up rage, kicking the bicycle rack . . . but proper competitors were supposed to be aggressive. If Nails really decided to beat Greycoats and co he would turn all that rage into beating them. The sparks would fly then! If he really hated them, nothing would stop him. The thought of debonair Seb Smith being beaten by spotty, horrid little Nails tickled Nutty's imagination. She liked it. She was only half-committed to the new idea herself, not nearly as sure about it as she had made out to Nails – heaven knows how they would fit in all that training, teaching three boys to ride! What had she said? She went back into school, brow furrowed, eyes gleaming. She felt extraordinarily excited.

Jazz, as she had guessed, was disappointed at the decision to call the challenge off. When he heard of Nails's interest, and realised the possibilities of the new team, he was in favour.

'It won't work,' he said, 'But I don't mind trying it.'

'Why won't it work?'

'Well, for me, I reckon I can run and swim, and make out on the shooting if I put my mind to it, but the riding – well – I don't know about the riding.'

'The little spotted horse is okay, probably the easiest of the lot.'

'It needs to be!'

'We'll get someone to help.' Nutty, overwhelmed at the success of her project, was beginning to feel the weight of responsibility. *Someone* would have to help with the riding! She checked with her uncle that he would keep them in horse-feed, and he agreed, amused at her presumption.

'That Nicholson lad'll be in the nick before next summer, mind you – and the sooner the better. He's always lifting stuff. Don't you take him home, my girl. You owe it to your parents to keep him off the premises.'

'Is he that bad?'

'So I believe.'

Nutty thought of him sleeping with the chestnut mare . . . Hoomey must have it wrong, she thought.

'That Miss Bedwelty,' said her uncle, 'she was hard on you, I reckon. Those horses, all right, I'm not denying they're in bad condition, but I did choose 'em. That big fellow, he were a class 'chaser in his day. Always had dicey legs, but with the rest he's had, and kids like you aboard – weigh nothing – he'll bear up okay for what you want. And the little circus horse, he's very civilised. He's old, but he's used to doing what he's told. So long as no one plays the National Anthem, he'll be fine. He lies down if he hears the National Anthem. That Miss Bedwelty – she's one of the green welly brigade, only think a horse is any good if it goes sideways and backwards – all that dressage lark –' (Mr Bean called it 'Dressidge'.) 'Manners, she says – but all you want is to belt across country for a couple of miles. Those horses, and four of you with guts – nothing to it.'

Nutty felt slightly more optimistic. 'You think?'

'You want to get that niece of hers – what's she called?'

Nutty knew that Miss Bedwelty had a famous eventing niece called Biddy who rode at Badminton and was sometimes seen clearing vast hazards on television.

'Biddy? But she's famous, top-class! She'd never teach *us*! Only for a fortune, at least.'

'She'd knock it into you in two shakes. Made of iron, Biddy Bedwelty. What a gel! That's what you want, not your old aunties.'

'If the PA won't pay for lessons from old auntie, they're not likely to fork out what Biddy would charge – even if she teaches, which she doesn't, as far as I know.'

'Biddy likes a challenge.'

'Well, Hoomey's a challenge. Getting him to do it.'

'These PA people – not asking for their money back, are they? The horse money?'

'No one's asked for it yet.'

'Well, if it's on again, and you're using your own pony, you've a horse to spare.'

'That dozy chestnut? Whizzo?'

'Offer it to Biddy then, for teaching you. It's the soundest of the lot, got good legs. The only one that has. Worth enough to get you started.'

'And suppose, afterwards, the PA says it's theirs?'

'Oh, I'll see you right, gel. Never get anything done in this life if you don't chance your arm.'

Nutty reckoned she was doing that already. But altogether her uncle Bean had given her the stiffening she needed.

'I might go and see that Biddy then,' she said. The prospect terrified her.

'That's the spirit! Nothing venture nothing win!'

What am I doing? Nutty wondered. I must be crazy.

'What's this about your school's packed in their challenge to us tetrathlon chaps, Gloria my darling? I've heard it rumoured, but nothing official.'

Sebastian Smith was nibbling Gloria's ear in the back row of the Roxy while the advertisements unrolled. Gloria was eating peanuts.

'The PA won't stump up the cash,' Gloria said. 'But Nutty says they're going on with it, whatever happens.'

'What's Nutty got to do with it?'

'She's in the team.'

'She's *what*?'

Sebastian emerged, startled, from out of Gloria's long curls and eyed his girl-friend unbelievingly.

'They changed it, she says. It's her now, and that beastly Nicholson boy, the brother of the original Gary, and –'

'You don't mean the swimming Nicholson?'

'Yeah. He swims.'

'Holy Cow! I'll say he swims! Are you serious?'

'Oh yes.' Gloria offered him the peanuts. 'And Biddy Bedwelty is training them.'

Gloria sensed that she had ruined Seb's evening. Instead of breathing heavily into her new hair-style and biting her ear lobe he was now staring at an advert for deodorant with a grim expression.

'That Biddy – by gum! That woman's –' He broke off, obviously disturbed. 'We haven't been thinking anything of it – that load of prats. But if what you say is true . . . My God, we can't go under to a shower like that – we'll never be able to show our faces again!'

'Oh but you're so strong, Seb! Don't worry. Have you seen that skinny Nails?'

'I've seen him bloody well swim.'

'He's horrible.'

'He can be Dracula for all I care. It's not his personality I'm interested in.'

'I'm sure you can run rings round him.'

'I can't swim rings round him, that's for sure.'

'Well, you'll have to beat Nutty! You can't let a girl beat you.'

The title credits for the feature film started to roll up. Seb put his arm round Gloria.

'I'm going to throw you over for your sister. Get her interested in the male sex. They say girls go off horses when they get to a certain age.'

Gloria giggled.

'Shall I tell her you're nurturing a secret passion?'

Seb groaned. 'That girl – once she gets her teeth into anything . . . like beating us, she's dangerous. You just keep us posted, let us know how they're getting on. If the worst comes to the worst, we'll have to go into hard training.'

'Poor old Seb! Give up sex and all?'

'That's right.'

'Poor old Seb.'

15

'By God, you've got a nerve!'

Biddy Bedwelty stood with her hands on her hips and surveyed Whizzo. He stood against the rust-streaked wall of the refrigerator factory, his thin tail clamped against the November drizzle, lower lip dangling. Even Nutty could see what an apathetic beast he was, and her heart contracted suddenly at the thought of their four stupid old horses going back to the knacker's. Damn Biddy! she thought. We'll bloody do it! The more people laughed at them the more stubborn she got. She knew that Nails, under his hard shell, was terrified of Firelight going. It was true what Hoomey had said: he did sleep with her. Nutty had gone up to have a nose, sat behind the oil-drum stack early and seen him leave. She had wanted to know how much it mattered to him because he wouldn't let on, and it gave her a valuable lever. Gary, evasively questioned, said that Nails was out all night at a girl-friend's house. He had told his father that. Some girl-friend, Nutty thought.

'I thought you said a chestnut thoroughbred? I reckoned about two thousand quid's worth at least.'

'Well,' said Nutty. The colour was right anyway, she thought, but didn't say.

'Are you serious?'

Biddy's gimlet eyes screwed into Nutty and travelled reflectively to the scowling Nails, nervous little Hoomey and Jazz in his rain-soggy turban, all lined up against the wall.

'Never ridden?'

'No,' said Nutty.

Biddy put her head back and yelled with laughter. It was an awful noise that made Whizzo shift his feet anxiously.

'And this competition is – when? *This* summer? Against that team from Greycoats? You don't mean it?'

Nutty hated her. She wanted to say, 'You beastly pig,' but didn't dare. It was all she could do to stop bursting into tears. After all she had dared, and suffered, and driven . . . and seeing poor Hoomey and mild, nice Jazz and temperamental Nails standing there listening to her *beastliness*, and it was all her fault.

'I do mean it!' she hissed. 'But now I'm sorry I asked. I'm sorry I've wasted your time. It doesn't matter.' Go to hell was what she meant. She snatched Whizzo's head round to go back in. 'My uncle said you – you –'

'Said I what?'

'Oh, he made out you were different, but you're just the same.'

'Just the same as who?'

'All of them!' Nutty cried out, stung by adults' crass thinking, wanting one thing, saying another, saying you had to when you didn't want to, and you couldn't when you did want, saying you were no good when you were, and good when it was something that didn't matter, like a pootling poem or something.

Biddy was looking grim.

She said, 'You *want* to do it?'

'Yes, but if you don't want the horse we can't pay you.'

Biddy stood glowering at Nutty. She was a wiry, muscly female of some indeterminate but youngish age, with crimped blonde hair and eyes as piercing as her aunt's, but green, like bottle glass. She had a presence that Nutty thought even Nails might appreciate, more nailsish than Nails himself; in fact Nutty, after her outburst, was frightened. She dropped her eyes, not liking the look on Biddy's face. Biddy did not speak for some time, and stood considering them in a way that made them all feel about half their usual size.

'I like a challenge,' she said.

Back to square one, Nutty thought. So had Sam, after several pints of beer, but a month or two later, sober, he had chickened out. She did not reply.

'If you win,' Biddy said, 'I won't ask for any payment.'

'And what if we lose?'

'Then you'll owe me for six months' work.'

Nutty's eyes gleamed. It meant they had to win. There was no let out. She looked at the others.

'The horses are going to the knacker's on Monday if we don't,' she said.

'Yes,' said Nails.

'What do you mean, yes?' Nutty asked him. 'I say yes, but it's no good if it's not all of us.'

'Yeah,' Nails said. 'For all of us. Why not? We got nothing else to do.' He fixed his eye on Hoomey, whose lip was trembling at the prospect. 'Eh, Hoomey?'

'Yes,' Hoomey whispered.

'Yes,' said Jazz.

'And what about the money if we lose?'

'There's my paper round,' Hoomey said.

'I can get it,' Nails said. 'If necessary. But we won't.'

89

'Very well,' said Biddy. 'Go and get your horses saddled. We'll start.'

Nobody was told the circumstances of Biddy's new job. It was arranged that they would take the horses down to the railway sidings where there was enough light from the warehouses to school in the evenings, and Biddy would come twice during the week and once at the weekend, for two hours each time.

Nutty found out that she charged ten pounds an hour. But there was no going back.

16

Getting Nails into the team did not make him any nicer. It was as if by revealing a hint of softness to Nutty, knowing that she suspected him of acquiescing in order to save Firelight from the chop, a girlish affection betrayed, he then behaved more churlishly than ever to make up for it. Nutty had hoped that underneath his Nailsishness there lay a heart of gold, but if there did he took care not to reveal it. It shook Nutty, for the fact that he adored Firelight surely meant that he must be nicer than he seemed? It was an obvious consequence. There was no one she could discuss it with, for Hoomey was too scared, and no one else knew. Nails slept at the stables almost every night, apparently going home for breakfast. Now that he was the official minder of Firelight, he did her before he went off. Firelight was conspicuously much less nervous, and when it came to the riding she did for Nails what she would do for none of the others, even Nutty.

'You do have an extraordinary rapport with this awful creature,' Biddy said, finding out the fact quite soon. 'What is your secret?'

Nails merely glowered.

When she made them swap horses in their lessons, he refused point-blank.

Nutty closed her eyes, seeing two iron wills come together on collision course.

'What is your reason for refusing?' Biddy asked.

'You're teachin' us to win this competition. I'm riding Firelight in the competition. What's the use of practisin' on another horse?'

'Firelight might go lame and you'll have to ride another horse.'

'I'll risk it.'

Biddy did not press him.

Nails stuck on Firelight like a limpet. She shied, she reared, went backwards, stopped dead from a canter, saw a ghost in every gateway.

'I'm not surprised she was for cats' meat,' Biddy said. 'It's not as if your task is easy, even with suitable animals.'

Nutty had lost half a stone since meeting Biddy. Biddy arrived on her Honda every evening there was a lesson whether it was snowing, raining stair-rods or shining frostily under a full moon. She expected them to be ready, mounted, properly turned out and willing. She inspected them under the warehouse light, her gimlet eyes roving over their grotty tack, the horses' condition, the state of their shoes. Uncle Bean paid for the shoeing.

'I want my money back if you lose, like Biddy,' he said to Nutty.

'Add it to the bill,' Nutty said grimly. 'It's only one thousand four hundred and forty pounds. A few hundred more's neither here nor there.'

Uncle Bean roared with laughter.

'I reckon with that hanging over you you're trying quite hard.'

Nutty was trying quite hard, the other skills coming with great difficulty. She wasn't the shape for running, she decided, although she was growing taller suddenly – too tall for her liking, because Midnight was only fourteen and a bit hands. The swimming improved quite fast once Nails decided to be a conscientious tutor; he swam beside her making her go just a little farther every time.

'But breast-stroke is useless,' he said. 'You've got to learn the crawl.'

'I can't do it.'

'If I can ride you can crawl.'

Nails could ride, she had to admit. Nutty practised the crawl in her bath and the water dripped down the light cord in the dining-room below and collected in the glass bowl-shaped shade. Three days later the ceiling came down. She practised sideways across the bed. Gloria told Seb, who liked it.

'All the same,' he said, 'Colin's swimming is pretty poor. It's one of our weaknesses.'

'Oh good,' said Gloria.

'Whose side are you on?'

'Me? I'm impartial. I spy for both sides. I'll tell Nutty about Colin.'

'Big deal. Tell her we all do the breast-stroke, refuse at water jumps, hit the bullseye once in a blue moon and get blisters when we run more than half a mile. She might slow down.'

'No. She won't believe you.'

'I've seen 'em, Gloria, with that Biddy crone down by the warehouses! It's frightening. Like in the cavalry, going round in circles without stirrups, old Biddy cracking her whip against her jackboots like a Nazi prison warder. The others – none of them could even ride a donkey, only Nutty . . . but now they sit there, knees in, heels down, on the bit –'

'Don't you do all that then?'

'No, only a bit before the competitions. We rest in the winter. I do anyway. I go hunting, but I don't run – too dark after school, dangerous me ma says – and the pool's empty.'

'The pool's empty?'

'Our own, at home.'

'Don't you go to the public baths?'

'You can't work there! Too many people in the way. Hopeless.'

Gloria reported all this to Nutty.

'They've all got swimming baths of their own,' Nutty confirmed gloomily. 'Colin and Mark and all. And at school too! Fancy our lousy school not even having a bath!'

'Perhaps they'd let you borrow theirs?'

'Huh!'

Nutty remembered past conversations with Seb, without optimism. It was true that it was very hard to work in the public baths. Now that she was doing the crawl (painfully) she barged into people all the time.

She passed Seb Smith's house one evening in the spring, taking a new route when exercising Midnight, and stopped to look over the hedge (too high for nosers on foot) into the Smith grounds. The pool was large for a private one, lying at the bottom of a vast expanse of immaculate lawn and surrounded by a high yew hedge which effectively hid it from all directions (unless you were on a horse or a double-decker bus). It had a sort of changing-room summer house, and a brick building that looked hopefully as if it might have something to do with heating the water.

Looking at it, Nutty realized you could use the Smiths' bath without the Smiths knowing.

She lodged this idea in the back of her mind for future reference. She remembered what Gloria had said about Colin being a lousy swimmer. One had to work on the opposition's weaknesses. Of their team, Nails was brilliant, Jazz becoming very good indeed, and Hoomey and herself working hard but needing help, such as Mrs Smith bursting out of her gate and saying, 'Oh Deirdre darling! Come and use our pool whenever you want!' Nutty rode on hopefully, but when she got to the gate Mrs Smith was backing out in a large yellow Range Rover and glared at having to give way to a mere equestrian. No sweetness and light at all. But Nutty thrived on aggression.

'I'll show you, you old bag,' she said to the back of the Range Rover. If Mrs Smith had been nice, Nutty's fighting spirit would have softened. If the whole business had not been impossibly difficult, she wondered if she would have bothered at all.

'There's something wrong with me,' she thought. 'Wanting to bother.'

Even Midnight's show-jumping had taken a back seat. Show-jumping seemed a potty sort of occupation compared with the one she was engaged in at the moment. She tried to think of life

93

without her monumental competition, and wondered what on earth she used to do, to think about. She could not remember at all.

17

Gloria said, 'If you want to use the Smiths' swimming pool,' – for Nutty had told her quite plainly that she did — 'friday night is your night. Mr and Mrs go to play bridge with the Fountains-Abbotts and Seb takes me to a film. The place is deserted by seven.'

Nutty considered. Now spring had sprung and the evenings were getting lighter the baths were hopelessly crowded after school hours. Her idea of using a private pool had become a compulsion. The Smith pool, she had decided, now refilled and sparkling blue, was shamefully wasted. She had yet to see anyone using it as she rode past on regular exercise both early and late: it deserved better. Nails thought it a good idea. 'Piece of cake, if we don't make a noise, even if they're in.' Nutty thought that was too much of a risk, but if they were out it seemed almost like doing them a favour, to patronise their pool, confirm that it was in working order.

She put the idea of Friday swimming at the Smiths to the others. Nails took such a proposition in his stride, unworried; Jazz, although slightly apprehensive, was keen because swimming was the discipline he most enjoyed and was making the best progress in; only Hoomey's eyes came out on stalks at the presumption.

'Well, it's you who need it most,' Nutty said. 'Every time you get barged you sink. You can have this one all to yourself.'

They over-rode his fears. He was instructed to attend on Friday at seven-thirty. There was a hole low down in the hedge that Nutty had earmarked for entry.

'Piece of cake,' Nails agreed as they lined up for the first time on the pool edge.

A thick hedge of cypresses hid the pool from the lawns that led up to the house. It was perfectly secluded, a classic ten metre rectangle perfect for training. They changed in the changing rooms so thoughtfully provided and came out shivering in the cool evening. It had not occurred to Nutty how accustomed they had become to the steamy swimming baths and the seventy-five degree water.

Nails dived in and came up looking shaken. With great restraint he said nothing. Hoomey took off as usual, holding his nose, and came up with a shriek that probably carried as far as the bridge party two streets away.

'It's *freezing*!' He plunged for the side but with three swift strokes Nails caught up with him and collared him round the neck.

'Get swimming, or else!'

Nutty stood frowning, not able to complain, her insides all knotted up at the thought of jumping in. But she had to, to establish her self-chosen role of leader of men. Dear God! . . . for a moment she thought of Gloria and Seb cosily entwined in the plush seats of the centrally-heated Roxy. With a despairing cry she flung herself . . .

'When you come to think of it,' she said afterwards, 'if you think of it as training, it must be far more toughening than those softy hot baths. We'll get on far quicker.'

The boys gave her dark looks, and Hoomey actually whimpered.

Nails shrugged. 'You get used to it.'

Jazz was philosophical. 'It'll improve – it's early yet.'

Nutty liked the implication that this was going to become a habit.

'Every Friday then? You must admit, it makes all the difference being on our own.'

They did. Nutty had reason to be optimistic about the swimming, for Jazz had improved phenomenally. He was a natural swimmer and loved it, and could keep up with Nails for several lengths with a long, graceful strike that far outshone Nails's for style. But Nails could go on for ever. Jazz's target was to stay with him for the full four minutes. He thought it was impossible, but worked at it with eager ambition. He knew he was disappointing where the riding was concerned, although no one had actually told him so – the whole business of being as one with the animal he rode seemed to elude him. Hoomey was better than he was. But the swimming both pleased and excited him with its demands.

Nutty told Gloria how it went.

'You swear you won't tell Seb? Promise?'

'No. I won't.'

'Where do they do their swimming practice?'

'That old Plumpton has them in the baths – an hour, private-like, once a week.'

'Private? Why them? You can't get it private –'

'Yeah, you can if you belong to the Club, and pay.'

'Oh, *pay* . . .' Nutty said heavily, scornfully. You could do anything in this world, she had already discovered, if you paid for it. She had asked if they could have it private, early or late, but had been told they must join the club, for which there was a waiting list and a subscription.

'Anyway,' Gloria said, offhand. 'They often don't go, from what Seb says. He says old Plumpton gets mad at them. And they're not all that marvellous. Colin isn't very good, Seb says.'

'Huh.' Nutty considered, and wondered if she wasn't perhaps setting her targets too high. She assumed that the Greycoats' team were all brilliant at everything.

'What night do they swim then?'

'Wednesdays, I think. Quite late. Nine o'clock. 'Cause sometimes I meet 'em afterwards and we go to the coffee-bar.'

Nutty went to watch the next Wednesday, to see if she could pick up a tip or two, and at least find out what they had to beat. The emptiness of the big shimmering pool in the artificial light galled her. Old Plumpton appeared in his white trousers and string vest and the four boys came out five minutes later, not looking keen at all. They all wore caps and goggles and black trunks and Nutty couldn't tell who was who. The professional look impressed her, and she decided immediately to get her own team similarly kitted out. Hoomey's trunks had green pineapples and monkeys printed on them; Nails picked up lost or abandoned (usually for good reason) trunks in the changing room and only Jazz had a reasonable garment. Encouraged by the vision thus conjured up, Nutty watched the opposition with narrowed eyes, and was pleased to see that, yes, Colin Constable, for all his smart appearance, was certainly not up to Nails's standard and not even up to Jazz's, although better than Hoomey and herself. The one she guessed was Seb because the hair on his legs was blond was the best, but even then not as fast as Nails, and the other two were in-between, but not nearly as fantastic as she had imagined. She felt much cheered. She remembered that Seb had said to Gloria that swimming was not 'their thing', but Antony Royd was supposed to run the fastest mile in the county and Mark Fountains-Abbot cheatingly borrowed his mother's eventer for the cross-country and just, according to Gloria, sat there. 'Knitting, I suppose?' Nutty had added sarcastically. They were none of them marvellous at everything. Which reminded her that they had done nothing at all about the shooting.

'Ask Seb how you learn to shoot, will you?' she asked Gloria at home, Sylvester having cancelled Brigadier Gatehouse.

Gloria reported back that, if she went to the police, they would probably supply someone. Nutty remembered supposing that Nails would hit a bullseye every time if he pretended it was a policeman he was shooting at, and wondered how she was going to reconcile that. Gloria then added that the pistols for shooting cost over a hundred pounds each and did she know?

'No!'

'He said he reckoned that would stop you.'

Nutty, having just thought the same thing changed her mind instantly.

'Nothing is going to stop me!'

Just four hundred quid to add to the one thousand four hundred and forty pounds, she thought wildly.

'Has Seb got a pistol then?'

'Yes. They all have their own.'

'Well, he can't use it every day. Not *every* day. Would he lend it, do you think?'

'What, to help you beat him?'

'It's supposed to be a sporting competition.'

'That's a bit too sporting, I should say.'

'Well, they already lend us their swimming-bath.'

Gloria laughed. 'Shall I tell him?'

'No!'

There was still time, Nutty reflected. The competition was to take place in August and, although she was for ever panicking about what they still couldn't do, she tended to overlook how far they had come from first beginnings. They could all ride now – after a fashion – and stay on over their modest course of jumps (built of railway sleepers); they could all swim at least three lengths and run a mile without stopping to fall in a heap every hundred yards, not very fast perhaps, but improving all the time. Jazz and Hoomey had stopped using the bus to and from school and ran together, fortunately down hill all the way there when they were always late. Nutty found both the running and swimming hard, but had no option but to keep up with the boys. She had lost three quarters of a stone in weight and found a waist, which encouraged her considerably. She skipped in the stable-yard and jumped up and down off orange boxes in the store-room and occasionally thought back to her carefree days before Sylvester went mad on their behalf. Sylvester was into darts now and had a school darts team. He did not enquire after their progress and Nutty forbore to mention it. She thought he was the dregs. It was Uncle Bean who provided the rock on which she occasionally rested, who kept them in horse feed and bought them the swimming gear she hankered after. They appeared the next Friday night at the Smiths' poolside looking fashionably anonymous and sinister like Seb's crowd, and jumped in eagerly, Hoomey obviously expecting his new look to do wonders for his crawl. His goggles filled up with water and he thought he had swum a whole length under water, and was so pleased that no one bothered to disillusion him. Nutty adjusted them for him.

Nails, sitting on the side with the stopwatch Uncle Bean had acquired for them, said, 'Jazz and Hoomey, three minutes. I'll time you. Start together.'

Each time, so far, they had made a little farther.

'I'll go when they've finished,' Nutty said, sitting beside Nails. Three were too many for comfort, side by side.

It was a warm evening, the first they had experienced, and the lawns smelled of lilac. The put-put of tennis balls came from next door but one, and cultured cries of enjoyment. Nutty felt very pleased with life, swinging her legs in the clear water as Jazz slipped past on his second length. Nails was becoming quite human, and looked positively Olympic with the goggles pushed up on his forehead, shouting instructions to Hoomey. The trouble was, a head mostly under water heard nothing.

'Save your breath,' Nutty said.

Nails actually smiled.

It struck Nutty that he had no time to take cars for joy-rides any longer, content to flake out in the thick straw in a corner of Firelight's box after evenings of running and riding and swimming. Although nobody ever remarked upon the fact, it was tacitly acknowledged now that Nails slept with Firelight; he had been discovered by them all at one time or another early in the morning still asleep. Firelight was now as gentle as a lamb, and would lie down and sleep beside him instead of pacing round her box all night.

Hoomey was splashing away on his third length when Nutty, getting bored, got up to fetch a toffee out of her blazer pocket where it was tossed down under the cupressus hedge. Just as she reached it, she heard voices on the other side of the hedge. Half bent down, she froze with horror.

'You've never seen the pool? We had it built two years ago. Come round and have a look at it – you'll see it's a beautiful job. We're very pleased. I thought Seb had gone out, but it sounds as if he's there with his friends.'

Dropping her blazer Nutty fled back to Nails.

'Mrs Smith!' she hissed. 'She's on her way!'

Nails looked up, his jaw dropping. 'She's playing bridge –'

'She's coming – oh, cripes, stop them!'

Jazz was travelling fast, oblivious, and the great wallowing on the far side was Hoomey's dying effort. Nutty sped round the pool, leaned over and screamed at him.

'Hoomey! Get out, quick!'

He looked up, open-mouthed, swallowed half the pool and submerged. Nutty leaned over and grabbed him. He flailed wildly in her grip and she pulled him bodily to the rail by a handful of flesh.

'The Smiths are here!' she squawked at him. '*Quick!*'

He lunged up towards her, petrified. She hauled him out like a conjuror's rabbit out of a hat. He stumbled, ran. Jazz was still powering up and down, deaf to Nails's pleas. Mrs Smith appeared round the edge of cupressus with a high-heeled elderly lady at her side, smiling.

'Hullo, dears!'

They fled, leaving Jazz to his fate. As one they plunged for the hole in the hedge. Nutty, last to disappear, was just in time to hear the visitor say, 'Why, how brown he is! Have you been to Madeira again over the holiday?'

They sped down the warm evening pavement for about fifty yards and then pulled up as an elderly man, walking his dog, came out of a driveway in front of them. He gave them a strange look and pursed his lips.

'What shall we do?' Nutty moaned. 'We've left all our clothes!'

'You go back for 'em,' Nails said. 'I'm not going to.'

He pulled his goggles down and stood glowering. 'Thought you bloody well said they played bridge every Friday!'

'They do – did –'

They stood undecided, dripping. A trio of skinheads were coming up the pavement, and some kids on bikes came by, saw them and started to circle back.

'Let's get the hell home,' Nails said abruptly.

'We can't leave Jazz!'

Nutty hesitated, looked back, and saw Jazz emerging bottom first out of the hole in the hedge. His new cap and goggles got hung up in the undergrowth; he pulled, got hung up again, jerked savagely and emerged without them, his long hair falling down tangled and wet to his waist. He sped towards them. Cries of, 'Stop! Stop!' issued over the hedge and dogs started to bark from neighbouring gardens. The skinheads broke into a jog-trot, grinning and whistling.

'You could've *said*!' Jazz moaned. 'You rotten lot!'

A bus was coasting down the avenue and Nutty said, 'Quick! Let's get out of here!'

She waved her arm at the bus, pelting for the bus stop on the other side of the road. The others came with her. The bikes closed in, whooping. Nutty had a glimpse of the bus-driver, pop-eyed, standing on his brakes. They leapt for the platform and shoved up the stairs in front of the people waiting, leaving their adversaries jeering and circling below.

'We've no money!' Hoomey whispered, shocked.

'We'll be in town by the time he comes up here,' Nutty said.

The bus was quite full and everybody was staring at them. Nutty shrunk down in her seat but, without clothes, there was nothing to shrink into. Jazz shook his head so that the hair fell down over his face like a curtain and sat looking like something that had escaped from the zoo, still heaving from his exertions.

The conductor came up the stairs and started collecting his money. He paused by Jazz, uncertain.

'You in there,' he started.

Jazz started to talk Punjabi, waving his hands about.

Nutty stared out of the window pretending she did not belong. Anything to get closer to home . . . stalling tactics . . .

'Fares, please!'

The conductor was tapping sharply on his ticket machine with a coin.

'I've lost my handbag,' Nutty said.

She dropped down and started groping round on the floor as the bus sped down the long hill into town.

'You never had a handbag, madam,' the conductor said heavily.

Hoomey was looking at her from under the seat in front.

'What are we going to do?' he asked.

'We'll get flung off in a minute, but keep it up as long as possible.'

Nails was looking out of the window as if he had nothing to do with any of them. The conductor bawled, 'Fares please!' in his ear but Nails did not move a muscle, nor make any indication of intelligence.

Nutty came up and said, 'He's stone-deaf.'

'Blind as well?' the conductor asked, and rang the bell to stop the bus. 'Come on. The sea-front – must be what you're looking for? Pile off, the four of you, or we'll go no farther tonight.'

'Can't you take us in to the Bus station? We'll freeze out there.'

'I recommend clothes another time. Get moving.'

There was no alternative now the bus was stopped and the passengers' amusement turning to impatience. They had to go. A cold breeze was blowing in off the sea which blasted them the moment they stepped on to the pavement. It was still about half a mile in to the town centre and, apart from Nails, they all lived more than a mile out the other side.

'We'll go to your house, Nails. It's nearest. You can lend us all some clothes to go home in,' Nutty decided.

They were all coming up in goose-pimples.

'Let's run, before we freeze to death.'

They ran.

'It's good practice,' Nutty panted, in a dying effort to keep up morale.

The first part, on the promenade, was not so bad as the last lap up into the town centre where all the local talent was collected round the cinema and amusement arcade or merely loafing about the pavement. There was no alternative route. Even Nails stopped in his stride as they rounded the corner by the cinema queue. Nutty got a glimpse of Gloria and Seb, jaws dropping, as everyone started to jeer and clap. She was exhausted and her bare feet were stinging cruelly, but to stop would have been fatal. Jazz padded up beside her, travelling smoothly – (he really was improving fast, she could not help registering, even in such dire circumstances) and muttered, 'Keep it up, gel. The last five miles are the worst.' He looked amazing, like Tarzan out of an old film, about to leap up into the tree-creeper. Nails was ahead but Hoomey was lagging. Glancing round Nutty saw some skinhead joker put out an enormous boot and trip Hoomey as he came by. Hoomey went sprawling with a yelp of terror.

'Jazz!'

Nutty came to an agonised halt. Jazz tossed his hair back for the first time to take in what was going on. The skinhead had his large boot across the back of Hoomey's neck and was standing making prize-fighter handclasps over his head.

Jazz went back and said, 'Lay off him,' but the skinhead lowered his hands into a more ominous position and said, 'And what if I don't, darling? Go and get your hair cut, you sunburnt poofter.'

Jazz clouted the skinhead over the ear so fast that the boy never saw it coming and reeled back, off balance. Hoomey scooted to his feet, but several interested parties moved in to deal with Jazz before he could make a tactful retreat. He disappeared in the centre of a laughing, jostling crowd.

Nutty screamed for Nails, who came back reluctantly but did not seem disposed to fight.

'What am I supposed to do?' he said in an aggrieved tone but (fortunately, Nutty thought) a misguided girl in puce trousers hit him over the head with a handbag and he launched himself instantly at his aggressor, being no respecter of the female sex, and thereby deflected a fair amount of Jazz's opposition on to himself, the girl's screaming indignation making her plight quite plain.

Nutty hovered on the outskirts of the melee not sure what to do next, all her team being gainfully employed in the argument and her own presence as captain obviously superfluous. Common sense told her to beat it while the going was good but loyalty held her, undecided. At this moment Seb came up and said, 'We know you're all raving, but you don't have to blooming well parade it, do you?'

'Oh, do lend me your anorak, Seb dear,' Nutty said, and he nobly took it off and handed it over. Nutty's morale rose a hundred per cent.

'And do save Jazz and Nails. We don't want a fight. We only want to go home.'

Seb groaned, but – with the impressive upper-class confidence in his own innate superiority which always impressed Nutty enormously – waded into the melee and started to beat off the boys who were dragging Jazz down the road by his hair. Nails and Hoomey wriggled free and made off like hares and by the time the opposition had refocussed on Seb as main aggressor rather than Jazz a police car was cruising to a standstill alongside and a new element was introduced. Nutty nipped in and caught Jazz by the elbow.

'We'll beat it now,' she said, and ran.

They escaped into the relative quiet of Nails's cul-de-sac and slowed to a walk. Nutty, hugging the fur-lined anorak round her suffering flesh, felt bad about Seb, but in no mind to go back. Jazz was limping and making pained, mutterings and cursings which she thought it tactful to ignore. She admired his courage in clouting the skinhead but he spoilt it by saying it had been instinctive and now he wished he hadn't.

'My father will be mad if he finds out,' he said.

'I thought he liked all that warrior business, you on a horse and your old grandfather and all that?'

'Cripes, yes, on a horse with a spear in the plains of the Punjab – not the same as in swimming trunks outside the amusement arcade in Northend on a Friday night.'

They gratefully made the front door of Nails's terrace house and crowded into the kitchen with the others.

'Go and find us some clothes, Nails – we're all starving, and I've got to get home and do Midnight.'

'Hark who's talking, all wrapped up in a fur coat; where'd you get that from?' Nails was indignant. He had very few spare clothes and did not like being found out.

'Seb gave it me.'

'Huh! Seb said his ma played bridge on Fridays. Seb –'

'Oh, shut up! Seb's all right. He'll get our clothes back, I bet. He'll come up tonight, I expect, to get his anorak back and I'll ask him.'

104

Hoomey's teeth were chattering after his dice with death; Nails's house was no warmer indoors than it was out. Nutty put the kettle on.

'Make yourself at home,' Nails said sarcastically.

'Thanks, I will. Find some clothes, there's a dear.'

Nails went upstairs and after a long time came down with a pair of paint-spattered dungarees and two pairs of jeans belonging to his father who weighed about sixteen stone, two jerseys of Gary's and a navy-blue suit of indeterminate ancestry.

'My grandfather's demob suit. I can't find anything else.'

'What's a demob suit?' Jazz asked in wonder.

'When you left the army. They gave it you.'

'Jeez, you must have been hard up.'

He put it on, abandoning the other garments to Hoomey.

'You look like a new religious cult from San Francisco,' Nutty decided. 'You only want bells, and a collecting box.'

'A shirt would be nice.'

'You'll be lucky.'

Nails gave him a drying-up towel to put round his neck. Hoomey put on one of the jerseys and the dungarees. The crotch came down to his ankles. The others got hysterical, but Nutty had to soothe him, pulling them up under his armpits and getting Nails to find a belt. The belt went round twice. There were no spare shoes in the house save size twelves (large) and Gary's track shoes which were too small. Jazz appropriated Mr Nicholson's carpet slippers and Hoomey had to make do with a pair of fluffy mules which the missing Mrs Nicholson had left behind.

'And if you want something,' Nails said to Nutty, 'You can go and look in her cupboards. There's tons of old woman's junk up there.'

Nutty discovered that the ex-Mrs Nicholson's clothes were all at least two sizes smaller than she was and mostly covered with sequins or beads of some description. When she had chosen the least remarkable and staggered downstairs in a pair of high-heeled purple boots the others got their revenge by wheezing about the room in hysterics once more.

'I'll ring up Uncle Bean, and ask him to come and fetch us,' Nutty decided, but the Nicholsons had no phone and the nearest call-box was past the cinema in the town-centre. And if they had to brave that to make a phone call, they might as well press on for home. Nutty donned her trump card, Seb's anorak, and prepared to leave. It had not, she decided, been the most successful training evening of all time.

'And those old Smiths might make trouble yet,' she sighed. 'I'll have to get round Seb, when he comes for his anorak.'

Jazz skewered up his hair with a few of Mrs Nicholson's hairpins and the three of them shuffled and clacked respectively for home, grateful for the now emptier streets. There were still the horses to do, and they would have trouble at home about the missing school clothes, needed tomorrow. Nutty felt depressed. She ignored the amazed looks that followed them up the long hill out of town, glad to reach home long before the other two. She thought Gloria and Seb would come straight home after the films, but Gloria was already there.

'Where's Seb?' Nutty asked.

'You're a fine one to enquire!' Gloria raged at her. 'He's in the police station, that's where, thanks to your crowd of raving maniacs. For causing public disorder or something.'

Nutty changed, and felt obliged to confess to her parents what she had been up to. They were furious.

'We shall have to go up there and sort it out, and you can make an apology. It'll be better than waiting to hear from them,' Mr MacTavish decided. 'I'll get the car out and you go and make yourself respectable.'

All right for some, Nutty thought despondently, thinking of the others in the warehouse feeding the horses, nothing to worry about any more. Just her to carry the can, the prerogative of natural leaders of men. She stiffened nobly.

Her father drove her up to the smart neighbourhood where the Smiths lived and parked his car outside. He looked gloomy and uncomfortable, standing on the doorstep straightening his tie. The Smith residence was a plush, elderly house set amongst trees and shrubs off the road; the lights were on and there was to be no deliverance. Mrs Smith answered the door. She recognised Nutty and lifted her nose a little higher.

'Well?' Her voice was frosty.

'I thought it best to call. My daughter has an apology to make to you, I believe.'

'Yes. Well. You'd better come in.'

Nutty had hoped that business could be concluded then and there on the doorstep, and stepped into the hall reluctantly. Hot from Nails's two-up, two-down behind the bus-station, she was resentful of this softly-carpeted, oak-panelled entrance. A wide staircase, also closely-carpeted, swept up to a gallery above, and all was lit by silk-shaded lamps with tasselled edges.

'You had better have a word with my husband,' Mrs Smith said, and indicated that they should go through into the drawing-room. Nutty's father advanced, but at that moment Seb appeared at the top of the stairs, grinned and said, 'Hi.'

Nutty stopped, and the others went on.

Seb came down and Nutty said, 'Gloria said you were in the –'

'Sshh! Not a word.' Seb nodded his head towards the drawing-room. 'I never let on. They let me go – I talked myself out of it. Said Nails started it – they know Nails. Least he could do for me.'

'Deirdre!' Her father's voice jerked her into the drawing-room. Seb came too.

'You are a rat,' Nutty whispered, her admiration changing to indignation.

'I could've said you. Count yourself lucky.'

Aware of further frosty looks from Seb's parents Nutty looked suitably repentant and said she was sorry for trespassing. Seb's father was a large, comfortable-looking man who did not seem disposed to make a fuss. He had a North country voice and said, 'No harm done, lass. But ask another time. Will you have something to drink, Mr – er –?'

'McTavish. Thank you.'

'Whisky?'

'A small one would be very nice.'

'And what about the young lady?'

Seb said, 'She's in training. It's not allowed.'

'In training? What for?'

'To beat me, father. In the tetrathlon.'

Mr Smith laughed. 'Well, if she trains anything like you do, she won't forego a drink for the sake of her sport.'

'But she doesn't, that's the point. She uses private swimming pools without asking. She's a fanatic.'

'Sebastian won't use our pool. He says it's too cold.'

'It is rather.'

Mr Smith laughed. He poured a couple of large whiskies and handed one to Mr McTavish who looked much cheered.

'You've got a cheek! Like us to heat it for you?'

Nutty blushed.

'What's this all about then? You challenging our Sebastian?'

Nutty was forced to explain how the situation had come about. Mrs Smith accepted a sherry from her husband and looked resigned about the outcome of the evening and eventually excused herself to see to the dinner, and Mr Smith poured more whiskies and 'something harmless' for Nutty which tasted delicious and brought on an amazing feeling of optimism. Their plight in Nails's house which had yielded such a bizarre collection of spare clothes seemed a week away.

'And so you're really set on pulverizing our bunch then? And with no help at all? Do your teachers know you are training on your own?'

Nutty did not honestly know. Nor did she care.

'That's real devotion! It ought to make you feel ashamed, Sebastian, to think half the time you don't bother to make use of all the facilities that are offered to you – you just take it all for granted. These boys don't know what it is to go without, Mr McTavish. We've spoilt 'em, that's the top and bottom of it. Now I came up the hard way, same as you. Nobody put themselves out to help me in any way at all, but I made it. Same as you have.'

Mr McTavish forebore to mention that he hadn't made it quite to the same standard as his host but was obviously pleased to be included in the generalization.

'Well, Deirdre's a determined girl once she's set her mind on anything, I'll give her that. She's a worker, and I like to think she takes after her parents.'

'She deserves to succeed. I'll see that you have access to our pool whenever you want, my dear, you and your friends. Come in the front way and make yourselves at home. I'd like to see you give our boys a run for their money. Make you sit up, Sebastian. Good thing. What about the shooting? How are you off for shooting facilities?'

Nutty told him that they weren't.

'I should think we could put that right for you. I'll have a word with – what's he called, Seb? –Sergeant Potter, is it? Got pistols, have you?'

'No.'

'Leave it to me. I'll get you fixed up.'

Seb was looking worried. 'Hey, do you want us to get beaten?'

His father laughed heartlessly. 'Do you the world of good! A bit of serious competition, just what you need. I'm very glad to have met you, Mr McTavish. I'll take quite a lot more interest in this competition now, and perhaps Sebastian here will get out of bed to train before school without being called six times – he only starts running practice about ten days before a competition, you know. Real Olympic material there, wouldn't you say?'

'Hey, dad,' Seb said feebly. Nutty began to feel sorry for him.

'Could I go and get the clothes we left behind?' she suggested.

'Yes, Seb will help you. Take her down there, Seb, and put the outside lights on.'

They went out together. Seb hunched his hands into his pockets and scowled down the lawn.

'After all I did for you! Wading into those skinheads – and that's all the gratitude I get! That's just like my dad – he's always on about what a struggle he had in the days of his youth and I get it all too easy. Just appeals to him, hyping you up like that. Make me sweat. With luck I'll break a leg or something.'

Nutty was genuinely sorry for Seb. He was at the mercy of crack-brained adults just the same as they were with crazy Sylvester. Adult logic took strange forms. An unspoken sympathy bound them in comfortable silence as they padded down the garden. Nutty was excited at the opportunities that had opened up, and finding out Seb's all-too-human frailty inspired her to thoughts of a smashing victory. Even marginal victory had never entered her mind save as an impossible dream. She wished the incalcitrant Nails was as amenable as Seb. Seb was a simple character compared with her star, Nails.

'You can see we can't stop now,' Nutty said, almost apologetic. 'It's just the way it's happened. It's all your old Plumpton's fault really, and Sylvester getting carried away. They landed us in for it between them.'

'Yeah, old Plumpton's always on at us, nag, nag, nag.'

'Where d'you keep your horse?'

'Mark's ma has got a livery stable – she's a real leathery Jane. Haven't you met her? She just gives us nags she's got there, whenever there's a competition. Mark rides her eventer, Swallowtail, and we have whatever's going. They're all top-notchers.'

'You mean you don't have to look after them?'

'Nope. We just go down for a bit of practice a few nights before.'

'They're all brought out for you, saddled and bridled?'

Seb looked slightly peevish. 'Well, yes. She's got grooms. And super jumps.'

Nutty was silent, her sympathy for Seb evaporating. The injustice of life stung her bitterly – Sylvester getting them Bones and co as if they were straight out of the champions' parade at the Horse of the Year Show and not even knowing that some horses jumped and some didn't, and thinking that all weedy little Hoomey needed was motivation to become Seb Coe the second . . .

'Huh!' she said.

'I can't help it,' Seb said, aggrieved.

18

Sergeant Potter called at the Gasworks and asked for Miss Deirdre McTavish.

'The captain of your Tetrathlon team,' he said briskly to the Head.

The Head gaped, and passed him on to Sylvester.

Sylvester said, 'I think there's some mistake. Our Tetrathlon team has been disbanded.'

'No, sir,' said Sergeant Potter. 'It has not.'

Sylvester weakly sent for Nutty. Nutty's eyes gleamed when she set eyes on the professional Sergeant Potter with four pistols in boxes and a load of shot and a thick wad of targets.

'Mr Smith sent me, said to arrange training sessions with you.'

'I'll fetch the others,' Nutty said.

'The others?' Sylvester said.

'Nails, Jazz and Hoomey.'

'Christ, you're not letting Nails loose with one of those?'

'Nobody is let loose with these, sir. That is not how we manage things. Discipline is everything.' Sergeant Potter was elderly and looked like someone out of Dad's Army. But his clipped tone withered Sylvester.

Nutty went to round up the others with the good news and returned to find their new trainer surrounded by an admiring crowd. The pistols lay in a row, black and gleaming. Some wag had already filched a target and pinned it on Sylvester's unknowing back. Everyone volunteered to try the new sport.

'Clear off!' Nutty said indignantly. 'None of you wanted to do all the other things, not that I noticed! Get lost, before we shoot you.'

Nutty could see that the three boys were so keen to get started she suggested they repaired there and then to the back of the bicycle sheds and had a go to see what it was like. The Sergeant agreed. They had to carry a table out with them, which was set up the required ten metres from the shed wall, and the pistols were laid out, and the targets pinned up.

Nutty did not take in much of what the Sergeant said the first night. It was the first time she had ever seen her team eager and willing and fully co-operative, the envy of all their friends. They hung on the Sergeant's every word, handled the pistols with reverence; their concentration was intense. The lesson seemed to pass in a flash. None of them wanted to leave.

'I can come down two or three times a week. And later I might let you borrow the pistols to practise on your own. If I find I can trust you to be sensible.'

They fixed two nights when they were not riding. That left two nights for swimming and Sunday off. Running was all the time. And exercising the horses now they were getting fit. In ten days Nutty had lost another eight pounds. Hoomey's thin arms and legs were hard and gristly; he was getting more like Nails every day. Jazz was streamlined and beautiful and started to attract the girls; he was the purest athlete of them all, but the more fluent he became at running and swimming, the more he lost confidence with the riding.

'We're all better at some things than others,' Nutty encouraged him. 'None of us is good at the lot. It's the same with Seb and co. As long as you can get round, you don't have to be brilliant.'

'But Nails has learnt, and even Hoomey's okay.'

Nutty suspected that the trouble was Spotty, rather than Jazz, who had started off with plenty of confidence, but now, because his pony was old and unwilling, got dispirited by its lack of co-operation. If Whizzo had been any good Jazz could have transferred but Biddy, having given Whizzo the thumbs down, had found him a good home with a nervous lady in the suburbs and he was no longer available.

Nutty discussed the problem one night with Biddy after the others had set off back to the factory. Biddy was about to get on her motor-bike to roar home.

'I think it's time we ventured out on to some grass and a

semblance of the real thing,' Biddy remarked, fastening her crash-helmet. 'I dunno where though, without transporting them in a lorry. Perhaps your uncle would help?'

'I'll ask him.'

They had done very little swapping of horses, mainly because Nails refused to and Hoomey, having become accustomed to the feel of Bones's hulk beneath him, was terrified by what he called the 'slippery' ponies – Midnight and Firelight – and could not make Spot move at all. Bones obliged him in everything he asked, even shaking him tenderly back into the saddle when he flew up round his ears or slipped tailwards. Bones was like a great bus and Hoomey had learnt to drive.

Nutty ventured her opinion of Jazz and Biddy agreed with her.

'Spot needs a lot of riding. Jazz wants something that will go on, like Midnight. But he's too heavy for Midnight. I can't work miracles. We've done well to get Nails and Hoomey going so well. Two out of three is a fair average. But, remember, the team is scored for the best three out of four. The worst score is disregarded.'

'But that won't be Jazz, not in running or swimming! He's very nearly as good as Nails. That's why it's all the more important that he rides well, out of us all.'

Nutty privately thought she would have the worst score of the lot. Riding was only a quarter of it. She went to shooting practice and scored three bullseyes in succession and felt a lot better. The boys were full of admiration. They went to swim in the Smith pool and Mr Smith sent a maid out with four shandies on a tray and several bags of crisps. Nails lay in the sun-hammock, swinging gently, while he timed the others at their lengths.

Nutty came out belligerently and said, 'Some trainer you are! Biddy doesn't lie in the grass telling us what to do! She *makes* us!'

And to her amazement Nails got up without a word, dived into the pool, came up alongside Hoomey and started correcting his stroke, bawling into his ear and galvanizing him into twice the effort.

Nutty began to think Nails was a reformed character. He no longer resented her; he spoke to her as if she were a human being and was occasionally seen smiling. He slept in the stables and was no longer touchy about the others knowing, although he was not often found out. Now summer had come Uncle Bean fenced in some of the waste ground for them with wire and they were able to turn the horses out, which made the work far less. He searched around for somewhere for them to ride out and try cross-country in earnest, and came up with some tatty farms off the arterial which were within riding distance. They sported ditches and hedges and he built them proper jumps in the hedgerows to practise over and life got far more earnest and dangerous. Hoomey, having learnt to steer his bus at a steady canter round the railway cinder track and clear two foot of sleepers on each circuit, now found himself with quarter of a mile of galloping grass and a hedgerow at the end of it reinforced with a telegraph pole. His bus turned into an Inter-City express without brakes and he sat on top and screamed blue murder. Bones bore down on the obstacle and Hoomey shut his eyes.

'My God, but that horse can jump!' Biddy said admiringly.

Uncle Bean, leaning on a gate watching with the resident farmer, said, 'They told me it was out of racing.'

'Reminds me of a horse I knew once,' the farmer said, 'long time ago. Won some races Newbury way. I used to go in them days. Broke down. I often wondered what becomes of the old fellows, when they break down.'

'They come to the likes of me,' Uncle Bean said.

'You sure your little fellow's all right, ma'am?' the farmer addressed Biddy.

Nutty was far from sure, and Biddy looked doubtful. Hoomey came back white as a sheet, speechless. Bones stopped at the gate only because Uncle Bean stood in front of it waving his arms. Hoomey shot up round Bones's ears and Bones, remembering his old ways, shook him back into the saddle and let out some contented snorts. There was a gleam in his eyes nobody had ever seen before.

'You've got a winner there, young fellow,' the farmer said.

'Fantastic!' Nutty said. 'You were fantastic, Hoomey!'

'Well sat, Hoomey! You were splendid.'

Hoomey's face, screwed up with panic and about to burst into tears of shock and fear, quivered with a heroic effort at control. He blinked rapidly, gulped.

'You rode him like a real jockey,' Nails said.

Nutty watched on tenterhooks as Hoomey took in his new situation: the centre of an admiring crowd. It had never happened to him in his life before. A shaky, twitching smile dawned, and he turned bright red.

'It was Bones,' he said.

'Oh, no, he would never have done it without you.'

Nutty realised afterwards that they had come within a hairsbreadth of total disaster. Hoomey had survived and, although terrified, knew he had to persevere. With the admiration surrounding him, he had no choice. Biddy blamed herself for the crisis.

'Who'd have thought the old bugger would come to life like that!' she said to Nutty afterwards. 'He knows the job all right. Must be an old chaser.'

But Nutty knew that Biddy's groundwork with them night after night round the railway yard had paid off: Hoomey could ride, although he didn't realise it. He just had to adjust to the wide outside and Bones's new top gear, hitherto unsuspected. After several more sessions out in the country, Hoomey got the hang of it, and learned that, even if he couldn't stop, he could steer, and that sitting on Bones's enormous flights through the atmosphere was comparatively easy once you got used to it, far easier than poor Jazz's problem of trying to stay aboard when Spot, cantering quite eagerly towards the jump, put his anchors out at the last minute and stopped dead. Jazz didn't. Time and time again Spot refused with Jazz. Biddy switched Jazz to Midnight, and Jazz got round all right. Nutty could get Spot over the jumps but did not enjoy it, and Biddy refused to let them swap permanently.

'It may be good for the cause, but the cause isn't everything,' she said.

'It is,' Nutty said belligerently.

'We've still time.'

'Not much.'

Three weeks, by the time this conversation took place. Nails's performance on Firelight was fluent and impressive. The mare trusted Nails and would do anything he asked. She would not jump for any of the others, not even Nutty. For the others she was still daft as a brush, nervous of her own shadow.

'It'll take another year to cure her,' Biddy said.

'It doesn't matter, if she does it for Nails.'

Biddy was a perfectionist. Nutty knew that without Biddy they would have got nowhere at all with their idiosyncratic beasts. Biddy wanted them all to be able to ride all the horses, but knew she had to settle for far less.

'Spot was in a circus,' Nutty remembered. 'Perhaps he'll do it to music.'

Biddy brought some tapes of circus-sounding music and Uncle Bean played them in his car, and Spot stood up on his hindlegs and Jazz fell off more heavily than ever he had done at a jump.

'Whose idea was that?' Biddy enquired.

But the music seemed to give Spot more interest in life. With music going full blast he jumped much more willingly for Nutty, while Jazz got his wind back.

'You'll have to get it on the loudspeaker when it's Jazz's turn to go,' Uncle Bean said. 'Pay the commentator a backhander.'

'What a team! It's not like this at Badminton,' Biddy muttered. But she would not give in. Spot was jumped to music and Jazz tried to feel more optimistic.

19

When Nails had the refrigerator factory to himself on a warm summer evening he felt amazingly content. He came back when the others had departed, bringing fish and chips or a hot-dog, and sat on the straw-stack inside the factory to eat them. If he let

Firelight out of her box she would follow him around like a dog. He gave her chips which she ate with great deliberation. He had a load of comics which he settled down to read until it was dark, and Firelight pulled at her hay and heaved gusty sighs and scratched her stomach with her teeth. Nails liked her company better than that of his father; his new way of life gave him considerable satisfaction. He no longer felt the need to borrow cars and go lifting round the shops to relieve the boredom. If they had known, people might have said he was a reformed character, but nobody had known much about his bad ways because he had worked on his own. He still took care to be rude and truculent at school to keep up appearances, but the old venom had faded. He despised them all anyway, especially Sylvester, because they had lost interest in the only good idea they had ever come up with — not, of course, at the time that he had admitted it was a good idea. Only when forced into it by Nutty, by the fear of losing Firelight, had he come to accept it as such in his own mind. And, if taxed by such as Sylvester, he probably would not now admit it in so many words. But fortunately his present associates in the adult world, Biddy and Knacker Bean and Sergeant Potter, did not waste time questioning one's motives like old Sylvester; they just got on with the job in hand. If he had not tried, they would have dropped him without a word. He liked this directness. He did try. Nobody but himself knew what it had cost him to start riding with Nutty as a teacher, and to get to his present standard on the crazy little mare when he had been half terrified out of his wits at the things she did. He had not shown how frightened he had been. Of being hurt and humiliated. Nutty had done it, for God's sake, and she was just a fat girl (well, not so fat any longer, but still a girl). He had to admit that she could still ride a lot better than he could. But even she could not manage Firelight, which brought him back again and again to the anchor-stone that Firelight had become in his life, which fact he would admit to no one and, in fact, had difficulty in accepting himself.

When his mind came round to considering this embarrassing enslavement of his macho male self to a mere animal, he felt at a complete loss to understand it. It might be okay for Nutty and even for a weed like Hoomey with his crass infatuation for the hulking ex-chaser, but for a cool customer like himself it was out of character. He had never forgotten the day in the bike shed when Nutty had told him the horses were going back to the knacker's, and the fearful panic that had exploded inside him, worse than any brushes with the police or his father, worse than anything he could ever remember. Blind, sentimental panic. He did not like to recall the indignity of it. Yet nothing had changed since, and his worry now was not for the competition, but for what lay beyond, what would happen to Firelight when he left school in the summer and joined the ranks of the unemployed or, with doubtful luck, got on to his father's building site. If he wanted to depress himself he could very easily, thinking on this subject, but he was not used to looking too far ahead in this life. It was three weeks to the competition, five weeks to the end of his school career, long periods of time by his reckoning.

Nails was generally asleep not long after ten, preferring to get up when the sun did, take Firelight out and clean up her stable and do his running practice before going home for breakfast. Firelight generally ate a bit of her haynet and by the time he settled down to go to sleep she lay down as well.

But this night the mare was restless. She kept walking round her box, sighing, and picking bits out of her haynet and dropping them on the floor. While Nails was still reading his comic, she lay down and got up twice, which had never happened before. Nails put down his comic and looked at her closely, worried.

'What's wrong with you?'

His complete ignorance regarding horses, except how to ride them, came home to him as he sensed there was something wrong. He got up, worried. Firelight came up and licked his outstretched hand, snorted sharply and tossed her head. Then she kicked up at her belly with one hind-leg and sighed gustily again. Or was it a groan? Nails became miserable with anxiety. He half-thought of going to Nutty's house, but it was getting late. She would be in bed by now, like as not. Her mother would be cross and he would feel stupid.

He thought Firelight was ill. Something was worrying her.

How could you tell if a horse had a pain? They did not go pale, or frown, or faint. He put down the comics and sat watching her. But then she fell to eating her haynet as usual, so he decided she had a touch of indigestion, and it had passed. He fetched his sleeping bag from the cornbin, where he kept it so the mice wouldn't make a nest in it, and curled up to go to sleep. He dozed off with the familiar, soothing noise of Firelight's hay-chomping over his head.

He was woken some time later by being kicked in the backside quite painfully. He sat up indignantly. In the darkness he could see that Firelight was lying down, but there was nothing unusual in that. But she was breathing very heavily and jerking her legs in a funny way, as if something hurt her. He stared, frightened, and she lay very quiet, as if kidding him. It was too dark to see her expression, whether it was sleepy or distressed. He scrambled out of his sleeping bag and went to fetch a torch he kept for when he wanted to read late, not liking to put on the light and get all the others going. They always thought it was feed time if the light went on and would scramble up expectantly and start pawing and whinnying. He came back with the torch and shone it on her. She looked at him, blinking. She looked quite as usual. He let the torch travel down over her back, to take her all in, and was surprised to see something peculiar under her tail. There was something sticking out.

Nails felt his stomach contract in a peculiar way. He felt both repelled and terrified. There was something definitely wrong, but what it was he had no idea. He thought she had a growth, or was losing her innards in some revolting way. Past visions of run-over cats and spilt intestines made his skin prick with horror. The mare's breathing was heavy and distressed and she kept turning her head round to him as if asking him for help.

'Christ, what's wrong with you?' he muttered, feeling quite helpless, and terribly frightened.

It was pitch dark and felt like the small hours; there was no sound of traffic from the road at all, and he was on his own with a vengeance. The other horses were asleep.

'Firelight! Be all right! You're not going to die, are you?'

There was no one to hear his pathetic funk; it really didn't matter what he said. The mare gave a sigh and a great shudder ran through her. She struggled a bit in the straw, and the growth under her tail seemed to grow suddenly while he shone his torch on it. His hand trembled. The growth was a sort of shiny, membrane-covered thing. Nails watched it with horrified fascination, and saw it start to slide towards him. The membrane broke open and he found himself looking at a little horse's head lying upon a pair of stretched out forelegs, a perfect little head with shell-like curling nostrils and a narrow white blaze, and wet, flattened-down ears. While he held this vision in the trembling torchlight, the eyes opened and looked at him, reflecting back the light of his torch. He was shocked rigid; even his breathing stopped. He actually felt his mouth fall open with the shock. And while he watched, Firelight gave a great heave and a whole lot more of the little horse slid out, its neck and mane and withers and then its whole backside complete with tail, spilt out in a heap in the straw, ungainly legs in a pale tangle.

Nails stared. For a moment he thought he was going to pass out. Although he now realised what the phenomenon was that he had just witnessed, he found it impossible to digest the truth before his very eyes: Firelight had given birth to a baby. Firelight hadn't been expecting a baby! Even Biddy, who knew everything, had never suggested such a thing was going to happen, and certainly Mr Bean nor Nutty had never said anything. Nutty had once accused him of giving his mare extra feed at night because she was fatter than all the others, but it was true: he did give her extra. She was fatter. She had been fat with a baby. Nails found his shock giving way to the shakes and the shakes to an immense compulsion to laugh. The little horse was the most extraordinary thing that had ever happened to him in all his life, appearing like that in the torchlight and looking at him even before it was wholly born, as if to say, 'Hi, mate.' It was now thrashing feebly about in the straw trying to get its tangle of legs in order, a whole, complete, new horse – when five minutes ago there had been nothing at all save him thinking Firelight had indigestion.

Nails laughed then. He squatted down in the straw looking at the foal, and the foal looked back at him, indignant, bright-eyed, quivering with life. Life! He had seen it happen, like a click of the fingers, the start of life, when the foal opened its eyes and looked at him. It was almost too much to take in, how it had happened so quickly, so unexpectedly. Nails was laughing and shivering at the same time, so excited that he felt almost ill with it. He was as trembly and thrown out as the foal.

'You little fellow, you ... you lovely baby,' he warbled idiotically. He had no idea whether it was a male or a female. He never really had noticed things like that about horses. He remembered that Firelight had to feed it with milk, but where she kept it he had no idea. As she got to her feet he looked underneath her, remembering the equipment cows had, and saw that she had a semblance of the same thing, although nothing like so dangly as a cow's, but quite satisfactorily dripping at that moment with what he supposed was milk. She stood over the foal licking it and nuzzling it and licking it again. There was the slimy membrane and some messy stuff that Nails cleared away diligently and threw outside; he got some fresh straw and by the time he had done that the foal was trying to stand up, with great difficulty. It could not control its folding legs, and Nails helped it, holding its backside up while it propped up its front end. All the time he had this great bursting feeling of utter incredulity inside him; it kept exploding, he kept laughing out loud at the memory of the amazing appearance before his very eyes of this whole new life; the shock of it would not fade.

By the time the foal had tottered and swayed and nuzzled at Firelight in all the wrong places and eventually found the right spot to have a slurp of milk, Nails was surprised to see that it was beginning to go light. He had lost all sense of time and place. It got light at about half-past four, he thought. The foal was lying down again and looking sleepy, and Firelight was dozing over it perfectly contented, and Nails decided to go down and tell Nutty what had happened. There was no point in trying to go to sleep again. He knew he never would.

He went outside, shutting the large doors silently and started off down the concrete road. He was in a dream, aware of the sharp, early air and the smell of damp earth, seeing the vast pearly spread of the estuary far away below him beyond the fading gold necklaces of the street-lights, and yet altogether apart from his everyday world. So far removed from normal sense that when he rang the bell at Nutty's house and her father came down in his dressing-gown thinking it must be the police, he did not understand the excitement.

'It's a quarter to five! Have you gone mad?'

'I want to tell Nutty something.'

'It's not the sort of time that people generally call –'

'It's not the sort of thing that generally happens.'

'Have you been up all night?'

'No. Perhaps.'

Mr McTavish, studying Nails closely, thought the boy was ill and took him into the kitchen and made him a cup of tea. He had never seen Nails before as other than a surly, rude boy, but now he was smiling and looked light-headed.

'You drink this and I'll tell her you're here.'

Nutty came down, blinking, wary.

'Are you all right, Nails? Dad says –'

'Firelight's had a foal.'

Nutty blinked again, frowned.

'You're joking?'

'No. I watched it come out. I *watched* it. You go and look. It's there now. It's lying there in the straw.'

Nutty was bewildered. Nails looked so strange she thought he was off his rocker.

'But you were riding her – yesterday. Nobody said – she –'

'If you don't believe me, go and look.'

But Nutty believed him, and the consequences of the turn of events gradually came home to her, and her face, instead of lighting up with joy, dropped with dismay.

'She can't!' she wailed. 'Not now! Not for the competition! Whatever shall we do?'

'Why?'

'You'll have nothing to ride!'

Nails did not follow, nor care at all. But Nutty, the disaster plain, was almost in tears of consternation. Her father poured out another cup of tea.

'For Gawd's sake, can't we wait till after breakfast? What a way to start the day!'

Nutty had to ring up Biddy straight away – ('Oh, well, it's getting late, it's five o'clock,' her father said. 'I daresay she's been up since three, being horsey.') Biddy, it seemed, was as horrified as Nutty.

'Come and see it,' Nails said.

'Whatever are we going to do?' Nutty kept saying.

She came with him, pulling on her anorak. They ran side by side, easy with training, breathless only with amazement, and now the sun was coming up over the edge of the sea and the whole world was sharp and glittery, concrete and weeds, and the barbed wire hanging drops of dew and spiders' webs. Nails felt as if he was bursting.

'Look at it! Just look at it!' He pulled open the doors of the factory.

Nutty looked, was struck speechless.

The others came up.

'What is it? What's happened?'

'That's happened,' Nails said proudly.

They were all late for school. Nails sat all day in a trance and every teacher who took his class reported his state to his form-master. Opinion was divided as to whether he was ill or stoned. He had to report to the headmaster at four o'clock, and was taken there by force by Foggerty who caught him racing for the school gates when the bell went.

'I've got something to do!'

'Yes, you have, lad, get to see the head, that's what you've got to do.'

'I haven't done anything wrong!'

'Just look at you, Nicholson. You haven't done anything wrong, perhaps, but have you ever done anything right? You leave school in a few weeks and you've got to make yourself a living. Have you ever thought what sort of a picture you'll make coming up before a prospective employer? Have you seen yourself in a mirror lately?'

Nails had to admit that it was true he slept in his clothes every night; he had bits of straw all over him and probably smelled a bit. He never washed, but considered swimming nearly every day took care of that. He had had nothing to eat that day at all and had been up quite a lot of the night and now felt a bit dozy, but it didn't mean that he was ill.

'There's nothing wrong with me!' he cried out in response to the head's question.

'Are you sure?' the head asked solicitously. 'Anything wrong at home? You know we can help you if you have – er – problems. The staff say you always look as if you've been sleeping in haystacks these days. Is your mother – er – back yet?'

'No, but that doesn't make any difference. She's been gone two years and you never asked before.'

'No, we have been remiss. I wonder if your father would like to come and have a chat with me, possibly about your future? He never put in an appearance at the parents' meeting. I would like to see him.'

Nails shrugged, thinking it highly unlikely. The head put a few notes on a pad and Nails was set free, leaving the two teachers puzzled.

'It seems to me that everyone thinks he's ill merely because he is less rude and rather more bearable than he has been in the past,' the head said irritably. 'Certainly the police haven't enquired about him lately, which makes a change. How's his swimming going? He used to be pretty good, as I remember.'

'He hasn't been to the baths for months.'

'Pity. Boy like that needs a sport.'

Foggerty, curious, asked Sam whether it was true that Nutty was continuing with her captaincy of a tetrathlon team: 'That fellow called with those pistols and told the head he'd come to train them or something. I told him he'd got it wrong. Do you know anything about it?'

'I asked Nutty and she was very evasive. Took the chap away and I've never seen anything of 'em since. But the funny thing is old Plumpton at Greycoats seems to think we've still got a team in training – something he said, about his boys getting worried. Made me laugh. Who's in this team, I'd like to know? I asked Gary and he said he'd packed it in ages ago, and so did young Bean. And Mr Bean's never said a word to me, so it's a bit of a mystery.'

'They get an idea, but when it comes to sticking with it, really working at it, they fold up.'

While Foggerty and Sylvester were shaking their heads over the modern young back in the staff-room, Nutty and her team were congregating at the refrigerator factory to take another look at the amazing happening. It was standing up, bold as brass, its long, stilty legs firmly planted, its ears pricked up, eyes bright, not frightened at all. They hung over the refrigerators, training forgotten.

'What you going to call it, Nails?'

'What is it, a boy or a girl?'

'What is it, Nutty?'

'It's a colt, a boy, stupid. It's got a thing, can't you see?'

'Where?'

'Where d'you think? Same place as yours. You are *stupid*.'

'I never noticed.' Hoomey went to look at Bones, thoughtfully. 'What's Nails going to ride in the competition then? You can't ride a nursing mother.'

Nutty groaned. 'It's ruined everything! Biddy said she'd come up here tonight. Perhaps she'll have an idea.'

Biddy came up with Uncle Knacker. They stood gazing at the foal, shaking their heads.

'They can still pull a fast one on you,' Biddy admitted. 'Not a sign beforehand. I didn't even think she was fat.'

'And she was going so well! It's a damned shame for the boy. I'll bring the lorry up in the morning and take her away.'

'Take her away where?' Nails whispered.

'She can't stay here, boy. Mare and foal's got to have a field of grass.'

'Where?'

'She'll have to go down in the fattening fields with the cows.'

Nutty looked at Nails and thought for one awful moment he was going to burst into tears. He was as white as a sheet.

'You can't take her away.'

Mr Bean looked at him closely. 'She's got to go, lad. They've got to have a bit of room to move, like.' He considered, still looking at Nails. 'Tell you what. I've got the use of a little field out by the Town Dairy. Old Carter's place. It's only ten minutes out of town. I could put her there if you like. You'd be able to visit there.'

Nails did not reply, but the pinched white look went out of his face. He shrugged, kicked the refrigerator.

'What are we going to do for a horse for you?' Biddy said to him, kindly for her. 'It's put us in a fix.'

'I don't care,' he said.

'Don't you?'

Nails shrugged again.

'Point is, you've got to care, haven't you? That's what a team is all about. Not just for yourself, you've got to do it for the rest. If it's just for yourself and you fall off and hurt yourself you can pull out, and nobody's the worse off, but if you're in a team you've got to get round else the whole team is in the cart. You've ruined it for everyone. So whether you don't care or not, you've still got to do it, haven't you? However much you don't want to.'

Nails scowled. 'All right. I played in the polo team, didn't I? They half-killed you sometimes. You don't have to tell me.'

Biddy was surprised. 'Polo?'

'Him and the Prince of Wales,' Jazz said.

'Water-polo, he means,' Nutty said helpfully.

'Oh.' Biddy laughed. 'Well then. You know. How long is it to the competition?' She appealed to Nutty.

'It's two weeks on Saturday. Seb says we're entered – he put us down. There are about ten other teams, but it's only them we've got to beat.'

'Why not beat the others too while you're about it? In for a penny, in for a pound,' Mr Bean asked.

'We'll concentrate on Greycoats first.'

'You come up to my place tomorrow night, Nails,' Biddy said. 'I shall expect you.'

Nails did not know where it was. Biddy told him. 'In fact,' she added, 'I'll come and fetch you on my motor-bike. I'll pick you up outside school at four.'

'And I'll go and fetch the lorry and take this little mare up to Carter's now,' Uncle Knacker decided.

The adults departed.

'What you going to call it, Nails?' Hoomey started again. 'You got to give it a name. Something like Surprise.'

'Dawn Surprise,' Nutty said.

'Sounds like a pudding,' Jazz said.

'Night Arrival. Midnight Express,' Hoomey said. 'That's a good one. You said it came out really fast. You –'

'Oh, shut up,' Nails said witheringly. 'You're useless at names. What about *Bones*?'

Hoomey looked hurt. 'He probably had a smart name once. I wish I knew what it was. Bones doesn't suit him any more.'

'Should think not, the amount of feed he gets through,' Uncle Knacker said. 'Never seen a doer like it. I'm off to get the lorry then. You can come if you like, Nails, as I suppose we can call you the owner of this new arrival. You want to see it safe in its new quarters.'

Nails saw Firelight duly let out into Carter's field with her foal. The field was not large, but it was full of good grass and had high sheltering hedges of hawthorn round it. On the town side of it, downhill, was an establishment known as Dairy Farm, and on the other was a large Victorian church and rambling graveyard. Exploring the area, Nails found a decent garden shed in a corner of the graveyard, well-hidden behind an overgrown yew-hedge, and he moved in there with his sleeping bag. From the open door of the shed he had a good view of Firelight grazing and she got to know where he was and would come up to the hedge close by and wait for titbits. It wasn't bad at all, although not as convenient as the refrigerator factory. But the fattening fields way down the arterial would have been hopeless. Nails had hoped Biddy would have foregone her offer to meet him out of school the next day, or at least be late so that he would have a chance of escaping her clutches, but when he came out she was there outside the gate on her motor-bike, and there was no escaping.

'I've brought my spare helmet, so we're all legal. Get on.'

He put on the helmet and climbed on the pillion. Biddy drove out of town fast, and down narrow lanes into the country of wide marshland and wider skies which Nails knew existed but had never set eyes on before. An urban lad, such wide open spaces made him feel exposed and uncomfortable. He was suspicious of the visit anyway, not wanting to change his ways. Without Firelight, the competition held no appeal any longer.

Perhaps sensing his reluctance Biddy was stern with him. She pulled up in a fair-sized stableyard attached to a farm which appeared to be miles from anywhere. Flat fields interspersed by dykes gleaming in the June sunshine spread as far as the eye could see and skylarks hovered and trilled overhead, but Nails, cautiously taking it all in, was given no time for comment.

'You need taking in hand, Mr Nicholson,' Biddy said sternly. She undid her helmet and shook out her frizzled hair. 'You think, just because Firelight is now out of action, that this competition is not your scene any longer. Isn't that true?'

Nails did not reply.

'And I think, after all the hours I have put in for nothing teaching you to ride, that you owe it to me to do your level best to win this competition. You *owe it to me*.' She nearly spat the words at him, her eyes holding his defiantly, making him feel very uncomfortable.

'I never said —'

'No. You don't need to say. Your lack of concern about having no horse to ride is quite apparent. The others are ten times more worried than you are. But you are going to have a horse, Nails, and you have two weeks in which to learn to ride it, and you are going to have to work damned hard, because it's a damned hard horse to ride. Do you understand me?'

Nails gaped. 'We haven't got another horse.'

'Speak for yourself. I happen to have half a dozen, and there is one, just one, that I am allowing you the privilege of riding, because I think you are capable of coping with it. Come with me.'

She put a hand on his shoulder and marched him into her tack-room at the end of the yard.

'You don't ride any horse of mine looking like a scarecrow. Put these on – I got some clothes that will fit you, and you can use for the competition. And this –'

There was a pair of cream jodhpurs and boots to go with them and a proper crash-helmet like jockeys used. Nails put them on because he had no choice, the mood Biddy was in.

'Now you'll ride my horse and we'll see how you get on. He'll feel a whole lot different from Firelight, I'm warning you.'

Nails wasn't quite sure what had hit him. Biddy's horse was sixteen hands high and a thoroughbred. It was young and inexperienced – 'like you,' she said – but, unlike him, full of spirit and raring to go. It felt like ten Firelights rolled into one.

'I know you can do it,' Biddy said unrelenting, and called for Nails after school every day on her motor-bike to subject him to another two-hour session on the aptly named Switchback. She schooled him on the lunge and in a fenced paddock over jumps, and then out in the fields and then out on the marshes, accompanying him on her own eventer and leading him over ditches and fences. Nails, getting the taste of it, stopped being terrified and began to keep his eyes open long enough to judge the thoroughbred's stride as he approached a jump and to know when he was going to stand off and when he was going to put a quick one in. He found it exhilarating – both terrifying and deeply satisfying.

When Biddy had driven him back into town she spent an hour with the others. Nutty was jealous of Nails's riding Switchback with Biddy all to himself every night but had to admit it had saved their chance for the competition. She could scarcely complain. Sergeant Potter had proved a godsend for the shooting, but the rest of their training was just a mess, the swimming and the running. Seb had stopped taking Gloria out and was to be seen every night with the rest of his team running in shorts and a singlet round the Greycoats' playing field, being timed by old Plumpton. But Nutty's team just ran when they were doing other things, like to school or to the refrigerator factory, and Nails ran up to Carter's field every night and down every morning and swam a few lengths of the Smiths' pool to get the smell of compost off him when the others complained.

Nutty lay awake in the small hours, worrying herself stupid. Nutty's mother worried about Nutty.

'You're driving yourself too hard, Deirdre. You're getting thin.'

This cheered Nutty up enormously. 'Have you noticed?'

'Yes, dear, of course I have. I was going to say, if you can find time – I promised you, when your father's insurance came up, you can have contact lenses. They'd be much better than glasses with this jumping across country you're doing. Why don't you go down to the optician's and see about it?'

'I haven't time!'

'But you do want them?'

'Yes, you know I do.'

'I'll make the appointment for you in school time. Then you'll be able to go all right. You'll have them in time for the competition perhaps.'

A month ago Nutty had had the wires taken off her teeth. All this glamour, she thought, would go to her head. She went upstairs and rifled through Gloria's things to try some of her make-up. She had some exotic liquids in bottles, one of which Nutty tried out and turned herself native.

'I look like Jazz,' she thought.

Gloria never sunbathed as she thought it was ageing; she applied the same effect out of a bottle.

'When this competition is over,' Nutty thought, 'I'll have a rest and be a lady and get a boyfriend and do ordinary things like everyone else does.'

She would ask Jazz to take her to the cinema. Jazz was looking very distinguished these days and was the only boy Nutty could remotely think of fancying. Nails, unlike Jazz and Hoomey, looked just as weedy as when they had started their training – so much so, in fact, that his puny appearance along with his new, apparent docility had set the school's pastoral care department into action. Sam Sylvester, deciding that Nails's home-life left much to be desired, set up what he called a 'tactful probe' into the Nicholson background. He discovered from Nicholson senior that Nails rarely slept at home and from Nails's classmates that he went off with a woman on a motor-bike at four o'clock everyday.

Nails, questioned, was evasive and, when pressed, silent altogether.

'If you will not co-operate, I shall have to get the Social Service people on to you. You are only fifteen, and if your parents will not take responsibility for you, and you will not tell us what you are up to at night, the only alternative is for you to go into care. You look like a ratbag and as if you are half-starved. It's for your own good, Nicholson.'

Nicholson then said something extremely rude to Sam, which made Sam blink.

'That attitude won't help, you know.'

Nails had half a mind to stay away from school altogether, but was frightened of getting his father into trouble. His father was violent when annoyed, and interference from the education authorities annoyed him. The violence, Nails knew from experience, would be directed at himself. He borrowed a new T-shirt from Jazz and tried to look a bit cleaner after his night in the graveyard potting shed, determined to keep out of trouble till after the competition. He was bitter about Sam's sudden solicitude. For once in his life he was doing nothing wrong. They hadn't bothered tuppence before when he was following a life of crime. He had enough to worry about anyway, without Sam's threats, for he had no idea what was to become of Firelight and the foal after the summer, nor himself either come to that. The thought of getting hung up with the council care people was horrific.

The others were no less nervous of the approaching day of decision either, although for different reasons. Apart from the question of winning, Nutty kept having nightmares about the money they owed Biddy if she chose to press the debt. Nutty did not think they would win. But the horror of losing was as much to do with money as with pride. Biddy had never let them down, come without fail all through the bad weather, and now was giving Nails an intensive course on her own horse which – in terms of money – was worth another couple of hundred pounds. Yet surely she knew they had no way of paying, should she demand it? Nutty dare not discuss it with her. There was a side to Biddy which they were all nervous of. She had not achieved her present status purely through luck and application.

Hoomey had long ago decided that he was the duff member of the team and knew that the worst score was discarded, and so felt that there was little onus on him. For this he was profoundly grateful and it stopped the worse of the panics. He was in fact almost looking forward to his ride on Bones. The farmer whose land they had been riding on had looked up his old racing programmes and had found the Newbury card listing the horse he said Bones reminded him of. It was called Bird of Freedom. Even Nails, Hoomey thought proudly, couldn't come up with a better name than that.

'And tell you what,' the old farmer said. 'It were a seven-year-old in them days, and look at the date on this card – ten years ago. And Bean tells me your horse is a seventeen-year-old. Well, why shouldn't it be the same horse, I say? There's no doubt he knows all about taking fences – you've only got to watch him.'

With this heady stuff ringing in his ears, Hoomey's confidence in his riding swelled out of all proportion. He might sink at the end of his eighth length in the pool and have to drop to a walk during his second mile, and shoot a fair proportion of his pellets off the target altogether, but his ride . . . his ride would have the spectators reeling with wonder. All he had to do was sit there. Bird of Freedom would take him. Not that he breathed a word of this to any of the others; it was enough just to drink it in himself, sharing his secret with the old farmer.

But Jazz was not facing the day with any confidence at all. As it drew nearer he became quiet and moody. He had seen the Greycoats' boys training and, for the first, serious time in his life, felt himself an alien. This thing he was putting himself in for was not ordinary athletics, but a curious hybrid of a sport which, it seemed to Jazz now, was so peculiarly rooted in the old British tradition that anyone pretending to come into it wearing a bloody turban was going to stick out like a clown in a gathering of clerics. The fact that he had little confidence in his horse did not help. It was not enough to excel in the swimming and the running, which he knew he did; what was going to be the good of getting good scores there and nullifying them with a duff riding round? The riding apart, he could have faced it more sensibly, but with the fear of failing there and the strange, intangible instinct he felt that he was altogether on foreign territory attempting the business at all, he felt more and more miserable as the day approached. This was not something he could explain to anyone else, not even his parents.

20

Nutty received the guff about the competition a few days before the date. There were ten teams competing and they were down as 'Hawkwood Comprehensive'. It was a senior event and although Hoomey at thirteen was strictly a junior, and Nutty and Jazz at fourteen were barely seniors, they all had to do a senior competition. That meant a two-mile run and a four minute swim. It dawned on Nutty, reading the programme ('Start 9 am prompt') that they had none of them attempted to do the four parts of the competition all on the same day, and she wondered bitterly if she would still be conscious when the results were announced.

The shooting was first – 'Before your hands start shaking,' Seb said cheerfully – then the swim, the run and the riding. It was to be held at Swallow Hall, by kind invitation of Lt. Col. Robert Sawbridgeworth, a stately home some twelve miles away. Uncle Bean agreed to bring the horses, except Switchback who Biddy would bring, and Jazz's father promised to deliver them on site at nine am.

Gloria said to Nutty casually, 'Seb and co are going to cheat if you look like winning. I heard them say so.'

Nutty was astounded.

'How can they?'

'I don't know. I didn't hear that bit. But they say it's not very difficult if you know how, as it's only a fun do, not affiliated or something, when you'd get struck off or something terrible.'

'Some fun!' As far as Nutty was concerned it was the most deadly engagement she had ever contemplated, to be fought unto death. 'Who's side are you on?' she asked Gloria, wanting to know. 'I mean, if you were to find out something that would make a lot of difference, in the cheating line, would you tell me?'

Gloria considered. 'It depends.'

'What does that mean?'

'On the day. I would like it to be equal. Fair, I mean – why don't you cheat too?'

'I don't know how.'

'I'll ask Seb, but I don't suppose he'll be stupid enough to tell me. In fact I expect he'll be mad I've told you that much.'

'You remember, blood is thicker than water. I'll kill you if you don't let me know what's going on.'

Nutty was trying to put in her new contact lenses, which she found very difficult. They slid about across her eyeballs. She could not make up her mind whether to risk wearing them for the competition.

'Suppose they slide round behind when I'm riding?'

'How can they? You could always go backwards.' Gloria giggled to herself.

'I'll take them with me. And my glasses. Then whatever I decide I'll be all right.'

'I'll put them in my handbag if you like.'

Nutty declined the offer, knowing that what disappeared into the depths of Gloria's handbag was not likely to surface again in a hurry. She had a sports bag to put all her things in: her swimming gear, her running shorts and her riding things. Biddy had produced crash-helmets for Hoomey and Nails and they were all keeping their fingers crossed that Jazz's turban would be allowed as a substitute, as for motor-cyclists; they had also acquired jodhpurs and boots second-hand (one pair from Mrs Smith herself) and a roughly matched set of yellow jerseys. Everything was in order.

On the day before – Friday – Nutty ordered them all to go to bed early, and meet at the refrigerator factory where Mr Singh would pick them up at 8.15 after they had got the horses ready. Sergeant Potter would meet them at Swallow Hall with the pistols, Uncle Bean and Biddy would arrive at lunchtime with the horses.

'Nobody is to be late,' she ordered.

She looked at Nails doubtfully, wishing he would choose a more restful bed than the floor of the garden shed at St Aloysius's, but his expression did not encourage sympathy. Nails had received a message from Mr Sylvester that the Social Services representative wanted to see him at four o'clock. Biddy was not coming and Nails had no intention of being around at four o'clock; his expression at Friday lunchtime was grim.

He left school before the last lesson at three, went into town for pie and chips, got stocked up with coke and doughnuts for supper and went up to Firelight's field. It was a hot afternoon and the first one for ages when his time had been his own until bedtime. Usually, what with shooting and swimming with the others and riding up at Biddy's, he had only got back to the garden shed in time to flake out until morning.

He lay under the hedge in the sunshine eating crisps and feeding some to the foal. The foal was called Bonfire and was splendidly nosy and confident and trod delicately all round him pretending that he was lying on the sweetest grass in the field. Watching him, teasing him, tickling him in the place he liked between his front legs, Nails idled the afternoon away, pushing out of his mind the horrors that lay in wait: the busybody care people poking their noses in, the job he had no fat chance of getting when he was out of school on his ear, no more riding at Biddy's, no nothing at all, not even any certainty of keeping in touch with batty Firelight and her pushy baby. He tried to pretend that none of it mattered, could half convince himself.

After all there must be something more to life than sleeping in a garden shed and having no money and nobody who cared twopence whether you were alive or dead (not after the competition, anyway – Nutty at least needed him till then) but what it was Nails could not fathom. Not given to self-pity, he heaved the problem out of his mind and tried to look forward to the challenges of tomorrow, but weariness overtook him and he retired to the shed and his mothy sleeping bag. He had a pile of comics there which he read until it was too dark to see. Then he fell asleep.

21

The police car, cruising comfortably up the long hill out of town, came to a halt outside the Gothic-Victorian pile of St Aloysius.

'This where you mean?' the driver asked his companion who was a young social service worker in a green track suit called Shirl.

'Well, could be. Will you come too? I mean, okay if it is the kid – the gardener said a pile of comics and old coke tins – but if it's a six-foot tramp with a ten-year-old IQ I might look a bit silly asking him about his home life.'

The policeman grinned, and got out to oblige. It was dark, and Shirl had a torch. They picked their way across the graveyard. A pony whickered from behind the hedge, and trotted with them. Shirl shone her torch and saw the stalky-legged foal, laughed.

'Look at that!'

It was not an urgent assignment, only routine. The policeman paused outside the gardener's shed and Shirl shone her torch inside.

Nails, suddenly awakened, could see nothing except the light. Panicking, he shot up out of his sleeping bag and charged. There was no other way out of the shed and quick moving had saved

Nails many times in the past. It could have saved him this time, but the policeman, half nerved up for aggression, caught him fairly in the doorway and hung on with professional ease. Nails, fighting and kicking hard, was forced into submission as the policeman twisted his arms up painfully.

'No need for all that. Calm down, kid.'

Nails calmed down enough to stop it hurting, but made it quite plain that he was agreeing to nothing.

'Better take him back to ask the questions,' the policeman said. 'Or he'll give us the slip.'

'We're not after you for anything,' Shirl said, quite kindly. 'We only want to talk to you.'

'I don't want to talk! I haven't done anything! Why don't you leave me alone?'

'We probably will, when we know what's going on. But you've got to answer our questions.'

Nails replied with some very bad language which somewhat alienated Shirl, and they walked back to the police-car in silence, and Nails was locked in the back. He was given no chance to escape, would say nothing at all as to what he was doing living in the graveyard and was locked in a cell at the police-station.

'We'll talk about it in the morning,' Shirl said. 'As you won't co-operate.'

When it was too late and Nails had had time to cool down, he realised he should have asked for Mr Bean or even Biddy or Nutty's dad to be contacted. But he was so scared of them getting his own father that he had given them no names at all, not even his own. In the cell he shouted a bit to bring them back, but only got shouted at in his turn by two drunken fellow inmates. Later a woman brought him a plate of bacon and eggs and a cup of tea, but said it was no good making a fuss now, it was too late. 'They'll sort it out in the morning, don't you worry,' she said, like somebody's granny. The bacon and eggs were surprisingly welcome. Nails ate them, wondering, distracted, what time in the morning? Nutty had said eight fifteen. The competition started at nine. The enormity of what had gone wrong struck him afresh and he started kicking the door and yelling again, but this time nobody answered, not even the snoring drunks. He heard the clock over the bus-station strike midnight. He lay on the bed, kicking the wall, sniffed a bit, swore terrible revenge on Sylvester who, he was convinced, had put all this into action, and eventually pulled the blanket over him. The police bed was the most comfortable he had slept in for years, and the meal really good. I could turn convict, he thought, and live in prison and it wouldn't matter then about a job or all the things ahead that looks so unpromising. But that was in the future. Tomorrow was what mattered.

'Jesus, I've got to get out of this place in the morning!'

He could come back later, but *tomorrow* . . .

22

Nutty waited for Nails until a quarter to nine, and then decided they must go.

'Why hasn't he rung up, if something's gone wrong? What on earth can have happened?'

Jazz's father made a quick swoop to the churchyard with Nutty but there was no sign of anything amiss, no sign of Nails.

'I deliver you, then come back and look for Nails again,' Mr Singh said.

There was nothing else to be done. Nutty rang up her uncle and told him what had happened, and then they departed. At worst, they could compete with three, but Nails was their star, their sure-fire big scorer.

'We don't stand a chance without him!' she said to Gloria, who had elected to come along too.

Now that the day had arrived, she had woken up, strangely, feeling full of optimism and excitement. The fact that all the problems were about to be dissolved, a result achieved one way or another, heralded in her mind a following period of perfect peace. Even if they lost, there would be no more to do, save blessed nothing. It was a gorgeous prospect. The day was perfect, hot but with a nice breeze. She felt she was positively looking forward to the day's work, until the dreadful anxiety started with Nails's non-arrival. Hoomey, from starting quite chirpy, paled as the awful truth started to dawn: that he was no longer merely there to make up the numbers. They drove in silence to Swallow Hall, and Mr Singh put the radio on loud to cheer the atmosphere.

Someone brought Nails a breakfast at seven, and then nothing more happened until nine o'clock when he was marched to a small room for an interview with Shirley and a policewoman.

Anxious to get things put right as quickly as possible he launched into his scheme for instant delivery.

'I was waiting for my mother. My mother's phone number is –' racking his brains, he managed to remember Biddy's number and gave it carefully. Shirl wrote it down. 'If you ring her – now – she'll come at once. Or if you let me talk to her myself, I'll get her to come down.'

Shirl looked sceptical. There was a phone on the desk.

'Okay.'

She gestured to Nails to use the phone. He was amazed at the success of his ruse, less confident when Biddy answered the phone.

'Biddy? It's Nails. Your son. I'm at the police station and they won't let me go. Mother, please come and fetch me.'

'What?'

'It's your son Nails, at the police station.'

'Bloody hell, Nails, are you raving?'

'No, it's the truth. I'm at the police station – *stuck* here – you've got to come and get me out . . . *mother*! Christ, Biddy – mother – it's gone nine o'clock! Come and get me out of here!'

'I'm on my way.'

Nails dropped the receiver with a sigh of relief.

'She's coming.'

139

A policeman put his head round the door and said, 'Shirl, you've got to see to the Palmer boy, remember. His parents are coming in ten minutes. They've just rung. And we want this room. You aren't supposed to be in this building for this sort of thing you know. We're always busy as hell here Saturdays.'

Shirl looked distracted.

'I can go,' Nails said helpfully. 'I don't want to bother you.'

Shirl gave him a scornful look. She went out of the room with the policewoman, locking the door behind her. Nails waited. The clock said nine-thirty. Nails found he was sweating.

At nine-thirty-two Shirl came back accompanied by Biddy.

'Mother!' Nails cried out, in case she hadn't taken her role in. Biddy gave him a decidedly unpleasant look.

'You are Mrs Nicholson?' Shirl asked.

'I'm Bridget Bedwelty.'

'Bedwelty? I thought you were –'

'She's married again,' Nails said.

'You are responsible for this boy?'

'It looks like it,' Biddy said heavily.

At that moment the policeman interrupted and said, 'Look, Shirl, sorry, but we've got to have this room. Can't you find somewhere else to sort out your problems?'

'We'll come back on Monday,' Nails said. 'Won't we, mother?'

'We have got to talk, but I suppose it can wait until Monday, yes. I've got so much to do this morning. I've got your phone number, Mrs – er – Bedwelty, and I'll give you a ring on Monday. I suppose you know your boy was sleeping rough last night, in a churchyard? We can't let this sort of thing become a habit.'

'No.' Biddy was trying to look like a repentant mother, Nails supposed. It struck him that having her for a mother would be a pretty gruesome fate.

'Off you go then,' Shirl said to Nails. 'Till Monday.'

Nails went out with Biddy who had her motor-bike parked outside.

'Thank you,' she said to him. 'If I'm your mother I must have been a gym-slip bride.'

'They never noticed.'

'Thank you again. That's because you look about twelve and act six. And teaching you and your friends has put ten years on me. My God, I took on more than I bargained for! If you don't do me credit today, I'll tell that woman a few home truths about you, my son, that'll make you wish you'd never been born.'

She got on the motor-bike and kicked it into its stultifying roar.

'Get on!'

Nails got on. As they sped out of town at seventy miles an hour his spirits rose. The sun was hot on his back and the police breakfast comforting in his stomach. Roll on, victory, he thought. Nothing was impossible.

23

Swallow Hall was a large Georgian house set in acres of beautiful parkland with a lake and lawns smooth as billiard tables. There was a private swimming pool behind the house in a heated, glass-walled pavilion and the shooting was scheduled to take place in a walled orchard beside the coach-house.

'Cor!' Hoomey said, looking at it.

Jazz knew immediately that he had made a terrible mistake. Not only did he feel coloured in this setting; he felt he sported green and vermilion spots as well. He followed Nutty silently, his heart sinking. Nutty was unhappy about the missing Nails, but did not seem put off by the setting. She led the way to the Secretary's caravan, chin jutting.

'If Nails doesn't turn up, we've just got to do it all twice as good,' she said aggressively. 'It's no good letting it rattle us.'

Lots of people were milling around the Secretary's pitch, harrassed-looking mothers and coaches in track suits and brash, muscly competitors. Nutty discovered she was the only girl competing.

'It's a boys' thing, I told you,' Seb said, appearing out of the mob, looking very cool and fit. 'You're only here on suffrance, because of your old Sylvester's bet. They won't let you make a habit of this, you know.'

'What, of beating you?'

'Of competing with boys, idiot. Girls' courses are easier. You're sticking your neck out.'

'I know what I'm doing, Seb dear. Just leave off.'

Gloria elected to go with Seb.

'Scab!' Nutty hissed. Gloria gave her a sweet smile.

'Hawkwood' was down to shoot at ten-thirty.

'We'll walk the cross-country course while we're waiting,' Nutty decided. 'We might not get another chance.'

After the swim, she thought, she wouldn't have the strength. The first team was already shooting. They watched, to see how bad they were, but their scores were quite respectable, in the seven hundreds. A thousand was maximum. Jazz and Nails had each on occasion got into the eight hundreds but more generally were around six and Nutty varied wildly between two and (once) a thousand. Consistency was not one of their virtues. They watched another competitor get one bull and two inners in a row, and departed.

'Probably fall off at the first fence,' Nutty said witheringly. The other two were silent.

Nutty wished desperately that Biddy was with them to give them the necessary encouragement as they went out into the park to see what sort of riding was to be required of them. She had said she would come as early as she could but she had her own horses to do first. The parkland grass was smooth and springy. Hoomey walked in a dream, seeing Bird of Freedom flying down these deer-cropped acres, ears pricked, back to the days of his palmy youth and the roars of the crowd. He smiled at the jumps, as if to friends.

'Do you feel all right, Hoomey?' Nutty asked him anxiously.

He smiled more widely.

Nutty felt it might be dangerous to interrupt his trance. Jazz looked as depressed as she felt.

'I don't mind the other things, but I hate the riding,' he said, gazing in despair at a wide ditch one was supposed to negotiate before jumping out over a pair of rails set at an awkward angle under some oak trees.

'You've got to feel confident, and kick on. Spot *can* do it,' Nutty assured him. 'You must, because you're our best scorer in the other things, you and Nails.'

God, where was Nails?

They inspected the course diligently and got back hoping to find him waiting but there was still no sign of him. Sergeant Potter was in the orchard with their pistols, but there were still three teams to shoot, including Greycoats. Nutty reported to the bossy lady in charge that they were one missing so far, and she said, 'You go ahead with three then. If he turns up he can shoot at the end.' She peered at Nutty through thick-lensed glasses. 'Are you a girl?'

Nutty declined to answer, outraged. Seb, overhearing, laughed and said, 'No one'ld know. You should take up a more feminine sport, Nutty, like knitting.'

Nutty made up her mind to change to her contact lenses as soon as the shooting was over. She watched Seb shoot and said 'Well done!' when he only got five hundred and eighty. He glowered at her. But Colin got eight hundred and forty and Mark got eight hundred and Antony seven hundred and forty. She had to admit it was quite fair.

By the time it was their turn Nails still had not arrived. They took the pistols from old Potter and lined up at the long table. Nutty switched off from her troubles, her old show-jumping training taking over: relax, concentrate. Shooting was concentration. Without Nails, she had to do everything twice as well. Her first shot hit the hay bales the targets were mounted on. Seb shouted, 'Well shot!' and got reprimanded by the bossy lady. Nutty put Seb's face on the target and got two bullseyes on his nose. Astonishment then spoiled her aim and she got an outer, and the same for her fifth shot. They shot five times, had a rest and shot five more. Nutty's halfway score was two hundred and eighty. Not good enough, blast it. Think of Seb, Seb jeering, Seb's aristocratic nose. She hit it again, got his ears twice, between the eyes once and his big mouth with the fifth shot. This added up to three hundred and forty, which made her total score six hundred and twenty, much better than she might have hoped for.

Seb looked cross.

'I pretended it was you,' Nutty said. Seb had only stayed to watch, and had to sprint off to the swimming-pool. He looked hurt.

Hoomey had only got four hundred, two of his shots appearing on Jazz's target, but Jazz had got a fairly respectable seven hundred. He looked slightly more cheerful.

'You know I'm no good, Nutty. I can't help it,' Hoomey said earnestly. It was impossible to swear at him.

'That's what's wrong with you, your attitude,' old Potter said. 'Your attitude's all wrong.'

Hoomey looked contrite.

'I'll give you some good talkings-to. You'll do better next time.'

'Next time?' Hoomey looked surprised.

'Let's get this time over first,' Nutty muttered under her breath. 'Come on. Swimming.'

'I can't do that either.'

Short of strangling him, Nutty thought, there was not much one could do with Hoomey. They collected their bags and made for the swimming pool.

'If we change first, we can watch Seb and co,' Nutty said.

There was no provision for girls' changing so Nutty went and changed in Lt. Col. Robert Sawbridgeworth's downstairs toilet, all pink carpet and gilt mirrors, and left her things there, emerging with a towel wrapped round her. Jazz, having swapped his turban for a cap, now felt much happier. The swimming pool area was crowded with competitors waiting to go and hangers-on and officials, and they joined in, trying to sum up the opposition. Like the shooting, it was mixed, some very good, some very bad.

'Nobody as bad as me,' Hoomey said.

The swimmers went in pairs. Seb went with Antony Royd, and they were both good.

Nutty sat glowering.

'I've left my goggles with my things,' Hoomey said.

'You'd better go and get them now then,' Nutty ordered him, not taking her eyes off the bath. How she would have to try! It would kill her. Four minutes was like for ever when you were in there. Even Seb and Antony started to flag. Colin and Mark, in white caps and goggles, stood waiting to take over.

Hoomey came back with his goggles.

'Who's in now?'

'Colin and Mark have just started.'

'No, it can't be them. Colin's in the changing room. I saw him.'

'Don't be stupid! It is them, it was announced.'

'Colin's got a double then.'

Nutty took her eyes from the pool and stared at him.

'You're joking?'

'No. Why should I?'

Nutty switched her eyes back. 'That's Colin, nearest.'

'He's swimming very well. Thought he was rotten at swimming?' Jazz said. 'You said so.'

The nearest swimmer was better than Seb. He had a smooth, easy stroke and looked as if he could go on for ever. Nutty remembered about the cheating.

'They've substituted someone else!'

She stared, transfixed by the treachery of it. No one could tell who was who with any certainty in swimming gear, and the judges didn't know them anyway. It would be terribly easy to switch somebody.

'How can we make sure? We must follow that one, when he finishes, get a good look at him. He'll go straight back into the changing rooms, I bet. Really fast.'

She was already on her feet, on her way.

'You can't,' Jazz said.

'No, you must. Go over there ready. I'll come . . .'

Seb and Antony were standing watching the pair in the water, just outside the entrance to the changing rooms. Nutty barged

145

through. She was pounding with indignation. Jazz, at her elbow, said urgently, 'You can't say – in front of everybody – not unless you're dead sure.'

Nutty hesitated. 'You'd look an awful fool if you're wrong,' Jazz said.

'You go and see if you can see Colin in there then. That would clinch it. And I'll watch here.'

Jazz went. Nutty stood close to Seb, who was still breathing heavily from his exertions.

'Thought you said Colin was no good,' she said to him, icily.

'He's been having special training.'

Seb gave her his bland, blue-eyed gaze, innocent as a new-born babe. Nutty knew, without doubt, that it was a cheat. She looked round to see if Gloria was there; she would know.

'I'm not stupid,' she said to Seb.

'What's happened to your star turn?' Seb asked her.

'He's coming.'

Nutty realised she had already discounted Nails. Despair flooded her. The judges were counting down the time to the four minutes; the whistle blew. The swimmer who was supposed to be Colin was halfway to the other end, and finished at the far end of the bath from the changing room. Nutty waited for him but, after a word with the official, he turned into the mob and disappeared out the other way. She had not expected this. Furiously she chased down the bath side, but by the time she had wriggled through the mob at the other end and out on to the terrace there was no sign of the boy. She stood fuming for a moment and then, defeated, turned back to find Jazz. Seb and Antony had disappeared. Jazz was coming towards her.

'I couldn't find Colin,' Jazz said. 'No sign.'

'Well, he was there, I don't care what you say,' Hoomey said.

'They've tricked us, and we've no proof!' Nutty stormed. She could feel her heart banging with frustrated rage, all her good intentions of relaxing and concentrating thrown to the winds. 'Just let them wait! We've just got to show them! I hate them! I hate them!'

There was no sign now of any of the Greycoat team. They went

146

back to the poolside. It was nearly their turn to go and all Nutty's strength had gone in rage.

'Gloria'll know, we must find Gloria!'

They were being called for. Nutty took off her glasses and handed them to her lane judge for safe keeping. Hoomey was dithering by her side; they were to swim together. Sink or swim, what did it matter? She was now so angry, about the cheat, about Nails not coming, that she leapt into the water with a sob of rage when the whistle went. Swimming killed her. She ploughed up and down, her breath coming shorter and shorter, her lungs bursting, her legs getting heavier and heavier . . . agony . . . she groaned, filled up with water, floundered to the bar.

'The whistle's gone!' someone screamed at her.

She could not move. Someone pulled her out.

'Are you all right, dear?'

She could not see a thing. She staggered to a bench and fell in a heap, coughing and groaning. Hoomey joined her, white as a sheet. Someone brought her spectacles. When she put them on she saw that Jazz was swimming alone. She steadied her gaze on him and the sight did her a lot of good. Jazz was a beautiful swimmer and was slipping up and down the pool like a brown otter, very smooth and easy.

'Look,' she said to Hoomey.

There was someone, at least to keep their flag flying. They were not sinking in total ignominy. He finished having completed twenty lengths. It was beautiful. Nutty hugged him and staggered away to the Lieutenant-Colonel's washroom where her clothes lay in a heap where she had left them. She sat on the lavatory lid for some time to recover, then washed the smell of chlorine out of her hair. When she was dry and ready, she took off her glasses and, with infinite care, put in her contact lenses. Her eyes watered and it took ages before she was sure she had got it right. They made her feel nervous. But when she looked in the mirror again, she could see herself beautifully – the first time she had ever seen herself clearly without glasses. She stood looking for a long time. It seemed to matter quite a lot somehow, although she would never have suspected it. She wasn't at all displeased with the

147

effect, and left the house feeling philosophical. What the hell? It was time she grew up and stopped bothering about these childish games.

They had not arranged where to meet, which was rather stupid so she went back to the pool. There were only one or two officials left there and one of them was saying, 'The only one missing is the fourth member of the Hawkwood team. We've got to wait for him.'

'He's not withdrawn?'

'No. He's shooting now.'

As Nutty was trying to work out whether this exchange had any great message for herself, Nails himself appeared through the terrace door, looking as if he had run all the way from Northend.

'Am I too late?' he asked the stop-watch man in his usual truculent voice.

'No. Get changed. We'll wait.'

'I haven't got anything – I'll go as I –' His voice disappeared as he struggled out of his T-shirt. He tore off his plimsolls and his tatty jeans and stood on the edge of the bath in his underpants, anxious and poised.

'Very well.' The adults were amused, patronizing.

The judge started him with his whistle.

Nutty sat on the bench, hugging herself with glee. It struck her then, that in all the time she had been training with Nails she had never ever seen him swim seriously, only loll about with a stopwatch or zoom up and down a bit to demonstrate to Hoomey or Jazz. He had never tried to see how many lengths he could go in four minutes. Now, Nutty presumed he had always known. He swam fast and furiously, putting in strong, agile turns and seeming not to tire at all. It was only a ten-metre pool and he did thirty-four lengths. The adults' indulgence turned to respect and when he had finished they all congratulated him. Nutty waited until they had had their say, noted the score and gone off for lunch, and then went up to Nails and threw her towel at him.

'Not bad.'

Nails turned round, startled.

148

Nutty could not stop herself laughing out loud, the relief was so marvellous.

Nails blinked. 'Nutty? Hey, you look peculiar –

Nutty said, 'I've got my contact lenses in, Not *peculiar*, you rat.'

'Oh, sorry. Is that what it is? Pretty then.'

Nutty blushed scarlet. 'Do you mean it?'

'Prettier, then.'

'Oh, all right. Why did I ask? Where've you been?'

'In the police station! All night. They came and pinched me. I rang Biddy and she came and got me out. I thought we'd never make it!'

He was half excited, half breathless, scrubbing at himself with her towel.

'How've you done? Have you all swum. And shot?'

'Yes. Jazz was super. And the others – they cheated –' She told Nails all about the mystery of the substitute swimmer while he got dressed, and they went out to look for the others.

'People like them aren't supposed to cheat,' Nails said.

'No.'

They found Jazz and Hoomey at the hot-dog van and there was a relieved reunion. Hoomey blossomed visibly. They went to look at the scoreboard but the swimming figures were not up yet and they were not too keen to see them anyway.

'Greycoats must have got a jolly good score, with that cheating,' Nutty said.

There were quite a lot of horseboxes lined up in the field nearest the road, although the running had to take place before the riding. Biddy had gone back to fetch Switchback, but Uncle Knacker's abattoir lorry was to be seen trundling across the grass with its big nameboard: 'Bean, Animal Slaughter' signalling his trade across the acres. Eating their hot-dogs, they went to meet him. He parked and got down, mopping sweat, cheerful.

'How are you doing?'

They told him.

'Your ma and pas are all coming up after lunch. I told 'em to pick up your fellow Sylvester on the way, show 'im how you've shaped. Give 'im a surprise. Do 'im good.'

They did not particularly approve, but did not object. The loudspeaker was calling for the runners and the first comers had already started, going off at one minute intervals from the gate into the parkland. The Greycoat boys were limbering up in a very professional manner (Colin Constable not looking the slightest bit damp, Nutty noticed) all wearing identical kit. They went off like Olympians. The four from Hawkwood stood slumped, with their hot-dogs, regarding them coldly.

'At least they can't cheat on this.'

'Perhaps they've got someone out there with a car,' Hoomey suggested.

'There's only the ambulance.' Nutty felt she could well be coming back in that herself. The riding would be a doddle after all this sweat and pain. 'Who's going first? You, Nails, you're the best. Then we can all try and keep up with you. Better than you overtaking.'

The returning runners were all in various states of agony, stitch, wheezing and slump and lay about the grass like the aftermath of a battle. Some could be seen in the distance walking. This cheered Hoomey up no end, as he thought he was the only person he knew who walked round about the threequarter mark. But Greycoats were steady and invincible. Nutty watched them in a rage.

'We've just *got* to keep going, even if it kills us. Look at them!' Like bloody robots, she thought.

Nails went off as if the police were after him, and Jazz followed. Seb came back, his eyes bulging, having gained half a minute on the competitor ahead of him, and staggered off to his mummy's car to be regaled with cucumber sandwiches and iced drinks. Nutty, last to go, advanced to the stop-watch man and gave her name.

'A girl?'

Nutty glared at him – 'pretty' Nails had said, and she cherished the memory, had already forgotten his qualification – and set off after Hoomey. She intended to get close to him and shout at him when he foundered, but he stayed resolutely ahead of her, spindly

150

and dogged, and she began to realize that she could well be the worst of the four if Bones did his stuff like a true steeplechaser. Nails and Jazz were splendid so far but Jazz was in danger with his ride. Nutty had a stitch already and realized that she was neither relaxed nor concentrating; she took a grip on herself and willed herself into a rhythm, fixed her mind on the job in hand. The hot-dogs kept repeating with all the various flavours of relish and tomato ketchup and she began to think she was going to be sick. 'Don't – be – sick – now – don't – be – sick – now . . .' she thought, wondering whether Hoomey was getting smaller because her contact lenses had slipped or because he was going faster than she was. Or was her mind wandering? Running was really awful, she had forgotten how awful after the first mile, when it hurt and the lungs felt like anti-smoking advertisements – the photographs they had been shown at school which had made half the girls dash to the cloakroom and throw up. But Nails smoked and he was out of sight. Yes, her mind was wandering. It was so much easier on a horse. What on earth had Nails been taken to the police station for? He never said. Was it illegal to sleep in a graveyard? Not that she had heard of. That's what they were for, when all was said and done. She felt she was well on her way there herself, staggering slightly as she came up to the turn which marked the last leg. About a hundred yards to go, and she hadn't caught Hoomey; he was finishing now. The last leg went on for ever, the field unwinding ahead of her like a prairie and her chest pounding, her legs like jelly, little black spots dancing up and down. The little black spots were the boys cheering her on. She crossed the finishing line and fell in a heap.

'Don't be so feeble,' they said, dragging her into the shade. Nails offered her a bottle of lemonade.

'Not bad for a girl,' they said.

She could not speak. Nothing would focus at all. She shut her eyes and groaned, and waited until she could breathe, and when she opened her eyes again she saw Biddy standing there quite plainly. She felt fantastically relieved, the duties of captain weighing her down as much as the actual competing. Biddy could be captain now, and she could merely do as she was told, which would be positively restful (especially on a horse).

'You've all got to ride like hell if you're going to beat those Greycoat boys,' Biddy said. 'In fact I think you've got to get three clears to win, unless your running was something phenomenal.' She looked doubtful about that, gazing on Nutty.

The others looked gloomy at this news.

'Have you walked the course? I hope so because there won't be much time if you've got to change and warm the horses up.'

'We have,' Nutty said, but she couldn't remember anything about it at all. Her mind was a blank. She would just have to follow the arrows and hope for the best.

They trailed back to the horse-park, unloaded the horses and got changed. Hoomey had gone into his trance again, gazing at Bones with starry eyes, but Nails and Jazz looked anxious and worried. Nutty saw immediately, as Switchback was led out, that Nails had something to worry about indeed, as Switchback was quite obviously not a novice ride, and a very powerful horse for Nails's puny frame to handle, a raking bay with long, alert ears and a definite air of wanting to get on with the job. Both Hoomey and Nails looked very small on their mounts, and Nutty knew that she and Jazz looked large on theirs. It was a motley team, their morale not improved by the sight of the Greycoats mob on workmanlike hunters all behaving impeccably.

'Well, it's up to you now,' Biddy said cheerfully. 'I'm going up the hill to watch, so I can see you go all round. Just ride them in steadily, there's no need to go out of a trot – they're steamed up enough as it is. And enjoy yourselves. It's a lovely course.'

Smiling, she had no cares. She went off with Mr Bean, who had two cans of beer with him. It was hot now and families were picnicking happily all round the course. Although not intending to, Nutty found herself riding over to have a look at the scoreboard, and she saw that they had fallen well behind Greycoats, and could only win now if Greycoats rode badly and they all went clear. Not very optimistic, she saw that there was no point in worrying. Only if the Greycoats made pretty good hashes of their rounds ... then would be the time to start sweating.

'We *must* do well,' she hissed at Nails.

It was unfair, because he had not let her down. He looked quite understandably nervous now at the job in hand and not disposed to make idle conversation. He rode by himself, quietly, and Jazz and Hoomey rode together. It struck Nutty then, as if seeing him for the very first time, that Bones, no longer bony, was now the powerful old chaser she had boasted about to Seb the night she had first set eyes on him: her boast had been more accurate than she could have known. His coat, his eyes shone, his step was springy as a three-year-old's. He thought he was back on a racecourse again, seeing all the people and the horse-boxes – stupid old nag! He was so patently happy that Nutty felt quite throat-lumpy, thinking of how he had come from Uncle Knacker's all scarred and broken-down . . . what did people *do* to horses? . . . and what, in heaven's name, was he going to do to Hoomey, sitting cheerfully on top with no more actual control than a fly on an elephant, should Bones get the Grand National bug when he felt the turf underfoot? Nutty began to sweat. She rode over to the start to see if she could see how others were faring. Greycoats were ready to go, looking unhappy, Nutty was pleased to see. Seb went off and fell into the first ditch. Nutty's heart gave a glorious bound. The others walked round with long faces, seeing how badly he was doing, and Nutty kept close to them, grinning, to annoy them.

'Seb's doing well!' she shouted, as his horse refused at the ditch Jazz had got depressed about.

Gloria was standing clutching her smart handbag, looking concerned. Nutty trotted up to her.

'They cheated!' she hissed. 'Didn't they?'

Gloria looked miserable. Nutty circled her ruthlessly. 'They deserve all to fall off. You can tell them from me I know they are a load of cheats!'

Midnight, not having been to a show for unheard-of-months, was behaving in a manner which made conversation difficult, and Nutty decided that she had better concentrate on calming down, or she would go the same way as Seb. He was now cantering back looking furious and Antony Royd was setting off at speed looking as if he intended to put things right. He went impeccably well, much to Nutty's fury, and disappeared out of view into a wood at the top of the course. But he was a very long time coming out, and eventually a fence-judge could be seen waving a red flag, which Nutty knew meant red for blood, i.e. ambulance needed. His horse appeared on its own and came loping happily back to its fellows. Nutty realised that things were really looking up, and began to get the panics, in case they had a chance after all. She rode back to the others who had pulled up to fraternize with the parents of Hoomey and Jazz who had arrived 'to see them win their prizes'. With them was Sam Sylvester who, Nutty was very pleased to see, was struck dumb, regarding Nails and Hoomey with astonishment. They did at that moment look highly impressive on their large, powerful horses in their bor-rowed clothes and Nutty was not surprised at Sam's reaction, knowing how he usually saw them. However there was no time to say all the right things.

'I think we might be in with a chance. They are doing terribly badly so far.'

Instead of looking pleased the others all looked as terrified as she felt already.

'You've really got to go well, and then there's a chance we will beat them. You've really got to try.' She kept her voice steady and calm, and pretended she was a great general going into battle.

Fortunately the parents all went off for the best view, taking Sam with them, and they were able to ride calmly back to the start in time to see Mark's mother's event-horse refusing three times at the first fence.

'They've handed it to us on a plate,' Nutty said. 'We've just got to win now. Three clear rounds and it's ours.'

Nobody replied, until Hoomey said, 'One of us needn't, if you only want three.'

Nutty quelled him with a look. She really did feel like a general, cool and determined. She just knew that she would get a clear round herself, for her feeling would communicate to Midnight and he would not bother to argue. If only the others could be similarly inspired! But to mention the sum of money they owed

154

to Biddy would hardly inspire them – as it did her. More likely freeze them in their saddles.

The Greycoats' team retreated to their horseboxes without looking in the Gasworks' direction, Colin Constable having finished with a mediocre round of some nine hundred points. Dismounted, they appeared to be having some sort of an argument, or at least discussion, and Nutty saw that Gloria was joining in. She had been trailing about with them all day. Traitor, Nutty thought. Perhaps she had joined with the wrong side.

'Who's going first?' Hoomey asked.

'I am,' Nutty said. 'Then you can go. Then Nails and Jazz last.'

She privately thought Jazz was the weakest of the team, and thought if the others went well he would be inspired to do the same. All he needed to get Spot round was confidence in himself to believe he could do it. Spot would go if he thought he had to. If he thought he could get away with it, he wouldn't.

The starter was looking in their direction.

'Are you Hawkwood?'

'Yes.'

'You're next to go then.'

Nutty gathered Midnight's reins up. 'You lot go on walking round. Don't stand still. Have them all ready to go when it's time, not dozing.'

This was the only test she was confident of, the only bit of the day she knew she was going to enjoy, accidents forbidding. After floundering up and down the swimming pool, wheezing across the running-field, this – *this* was the bit where she came into her own. She rode down to the starter and Midnight started to prance about in his usual fashion, raring to go.

The starter looked at his stop-watch.

'Off you go!'

It was not a race, and the time allowed was generous enough, but Midnight did nothing by halves and Nutty's feeling, as she was signalled away, was of a magnificent release. She laughed as they flew over the dry springy turf, and the jump where the Fountains-Abbot's eventer declined to compete was behind her with scarcely a lengthening of the pony's stride. The course was easy enough – or seemed so the way she felt – across the next field and into the big ditch which Jazz had looked gloomy about . . . but it was potty! Up and out over the rails with a twitch of his black tail, Midnight made nothing of it, and was pulling madly for the wood where Antony Royd had come to grief. There were two big log piles to negotiate, and then fast down a peaty ride to the low gate out, all of which Midnight flew.

The parkland beyond sloped away downhill to where, about a mile away, the big arterial into Northend cut a swathe through the countryside. Nutty saw the distant trail of lorries and cars like a toy-shop model, shimmering through a heat-haze, but her way was right-handed, swinging away over an easy jump of straw-bales towards a slip-rail set in the line of the hedge, which had to be taken down, dismounted, and put back after leading through. All right if you could stop . . . Nutty guessed Hoomey and Nails would have trouble here, especially getting back on, although they had practised enough, especially Hoomey. Nobody said, Biddy had pointed out, that you could not climb on the rail once you had put it back and mount from there – that is, if the horse was inclined to wait for you. That was the trouble . . . once steamed up with plenty of galloping behind them, horses could not be bothered to stand still and fiddle about with stupid slip-rails or gates, anxious to get on with it. But Midnight found there was no mistaking Nutty's intentions: that the slip-rail was not for jumping. He came to a reluctant halt in about three strides which almost pitched Nutty out of the saddle without the bother of dismounting.

The judge's car parked beside the obstacle was the Mercedes belonging to the eventing Mrs Fountains-Abbott, Nutty noticed, and leathery Jane herself was timing their passage through the gap. She looked cross, no doubt mulling on her own horse's failure to get round, and glared at Nutty as she put the rail back in its holder in a very creditable time – nobody, Nutty thought, could have done it quicker . . . Midnight was off while she still had only one foot in the stirrup, but no harm done, belting downhill towards a trio of lovely inviting jumps dotted out in the open, no problem. Nutty was singing and grinning to herself, had time to realise that her contact lenses were doing splendidly, not slipped round at all, and everything was quite as large as life and clear as crystal . . . even three enormous telegraph poles which in cold blood she would have felt quite nervous of, but whoosh! – Midnight stood off like a chaser and cleared them by miles. She was on her way home now, no slackening of the keen gallop, only the beastly gate to stop for again – how these course-builders did like to hold up the action, when it would have been so much simpler to fly it! Brakes, brakes, Midnight! She lurched to another reluctant halt. This time one did not dismount, but prayed that the pony would stand still in the right place long enough for its rider to undo the latch. Yes, not bad. Midnight did know about gates and condescended to wait for Nutty to put the latch back, although not without a lot of snorting and blowing and crunching of the bit with impatience. It was a very smart performance. Nutty trusted Seb was watching through his mummy's binoculars and grinding his teeth as hard as Midnight, not with impatience but with rage.

She went back over the last two jumps and through the finish, fast and clear. Hoomey was waiting to go, looking both petrified and mad-keen to be away, his eyes shining with the strange fanatical gleam that came into them at such moments with his darling Bones. Darling Bones looked strong and was completely in charge, Nutty could see at a glance.

'Hold on! Good luck!'

Hoomey was away, Bones tearing the reins out of his frail little hands. Nutty's heart went with him. He'll never stop, she thought frantically! Not till Bones thought he could hear the roar of the crowds in the stands, which would certainly not be out on the lonely top of the hill where leathery Jane stood with her stop-watch. At that moment, Nutty scented disaster. She dismounted, her own marvellous round already pushed behind her. Nails and Jazz had pulled up and were watching Hoomey go, somewhat nervously.

To Nutty's surprise, Gloria was waiting to receive her.

'You did jolly well,' she said, 'much better than any of that lot.' Gloria jerked her head back towards the horse-boxes.

'They did cheat, didn't they?' Nutty said sternly.

'I came to tell you they're going to cheat again.'

'How can they?'

'They had it planned, in case it was needed, and now they've decided it is, because they rode so badly. So I thought it only fair to tell you. If they got away with one cheat, it's your turn to know about the other one.'

'What *are* you talking about?'

Nutty had dismounted, after seeing Hoomey out of sight, and now stood with Nails and Jazz who were taking an apprehensive interest in Gloria's babble.

'They've got a record of "God Save the Queen" in leathery Jane's Mercedes, and when Spot goes through the slip rail Mark's brother is going to turn it on, loud.'

'So he'll lie down!'

'Jeez, that's all I need,' Jazz said.

'*You* told them he did that!' Nutty turned on her sister furiously. 'You needn't have told them that – that's real treachery! That's –'

'I told them ages ago! I'd forgotten it myself! It's really mean, that's why I've come and warned you. I've done my best.' Gloria looked contrite, even distressed, but Nutty was too far gone to forgive anything.

She turned to Jazz. 'You're going last. If Hoomey and Nails go okay, it doesn't matter!'

'Where is Hoomey?' Nails said tightly.

'He's gone into the wood, out of sight,' Nutty said.

'He should've appeared again by now, the rate he was going.'

Nutty turned her gaze to the hilltop out of the wood where from the start there was a glimpse of a competitor before it took the long loop round the straw-bales towards the slip-rail. Of Hoomey no glimpse. Rather, there seemed to be activity of a different sort, people running about waving their arms. Then, ominously, from the fence-judge, a waving of flags, not only the red for blood but the white for course-builder, vet and all available emergencies. Land-Rovers were set in motion, one coming downhill no doubt with a message, and others going up to meet it. Earnest confabulations and waving of arms.

Nutty discounted Hoomey.

'Jazz has got to make it now,' she said grimly. 'You, Nails, and Jazz, you've got to do clears.'

She hadn't done her magnificent effort to see it all go down the drain now.

If Jazz could have looked pale, Nutty knew that he would have. If Spot was to be got round by pure will and determination, Nutty could see that the required elements were missing, and no captain-like exhortations of hers were going to instil them now, especially after the news of 'God Save the Queen'.

Nutty thought fast. In her present mood she knew *she* could get Spot round. She could get a donkey round, if it mattered that much. But that was against the rules. So was the same horse going round twice.

'Colin cheated. He didn't swim. You needn't ride, Jazz. *I'll* ride Spot. And that will make us quits.' She spoke in a low voice, but the urgency transfixed them.

'You can't!' Gloria squeaked. 'How can –'

'You're the wrong colour,' Nails said.

'That stuff you've got, Gloria,' Nutty gabbled frantically. 'In your handbag – the Glamour-Bronze, or whatever it's called – that, and Jazz's turban – no one'll know, for heaven's sake, as long as I don't get near the starter. Come on – we can do it in the horse-box. Hurry, hurry!'

They all looked stunned. Nails, next to go when the emergency squadrons had cleared the course and Hoomey's fate was made plain, had to stay by the start, but the rest of them galloped across to the abattoir lorry. There was no time to lose, no time for second thoughts.

Jazz was thrilled to be delivered from what he was dreading, but sceptical of Nutty's attempts at disguise. Gloria turned the whole contents of her handbag out on the horse-box floor, and found the tube of Glamour-Bronze.

'God, am I that colour?' Jazz asked, appalled.

'Shut up, and give me your turban,' Nutty muttered. Gloria was applying the Glamour-Bronze with abandon.

'At least you haven't got to wear your specs. That would've been a dead give-away!'

'Has Nails started yet?'

'No.'

'*Whatever* happened to Hoomey?'

Gloria was smoothing Nutty's Indian tan as best she could while Nutty was trying to push up stray curls under the turban. There was nothing else to put on, for their clothes were identical.

'Except you've got a bosom,' Jazz said.

Nutty hunched her shoulders. 'S'nothing like Gloria's. It won't show, if I keep bent.'

'You could squash it down with a tail bandage,' Gloria suggested helpfully.

'No. Nails has started. There won't be time,' Jazz said.

'Oh, I must watch! Where's Hoomey got to, for heaven's sake? Do I look all right? Do I look like you, Jazz?'

'Cripes, I hope I don't look like that, that's all,' Jazz said fervently. 'I suppose, if you gallop flat out and they're all blind as bats out there, it might work.'

'You stay hidden here, whatever happens, and when I get back I'll come straight back here and we'll swap back, before anyone talks to me or anything. But stay hidden. Don't let any Greycoats see you!'

'What about "God Save the Queen"?'

Nutty shrugged. If she got that far she'd worry about it then. 'God save us all, as far as I'm concerned. Hope Nails is okay!'

She went outside and got on to Spot and rode him sharply down towards the starter, trying to instil a sense of urgency. Not too close to the starter. She saw Nails go past on the top of the hill out of the wood, still in one piece, but still no sign of Hoomey. But if the course was operating again, presumably he wasn't a corpse somewhere, else the day's sport would have been abandoned out of decency. No doubt Bones was still galloping about looking for the grandstand.

Nails must have been going well, for she was given the office to start before he was back in sight. The starter did not seem to have divined her secret – perhaps a glance showed a mere spotted pony, which had been standing around for the last twenty minutes and had a turban on top, so why look farther? Nutty got Spot into a surprised gallop and hurtled through the start as she determined to go on. She did not want any fence-judge to get a closer look than was necessary and speed was all. Spot, never fast, had got the message and was progressing at a commendable pace, and Nutty gave him no time to think twice approaching the first jumps, but hustled him on with busy heels. Treated in that way, which sprung from the rider's own confidence, he found it less arduous to jump than to refuse. They reached the wood without incident, and from the top of the hill Nutty got a glimpse of Nails haring down towards the finish, looking as if he had done a fast time, which spurred her on for they were still in with a chance. Discounting Hoomey, three clears were still a possibility.

The turban gave her a muffled feel, covering her ears, and she was terrified she would spike it on overhanging brambles through the wood and be revealed on the far side, her Glamour-Bronze stopping in a hard line well clear of her hair. She held it on with one hand over the log piles, the general gloom of the wood making her feel much safer from the fence-judge's eye than the sunlight outside, and emerged unscathed into the top of the park, where she found the emergency vehicles parked with the knot of summoned officials gathered round, all gazing down the hill.

Wanting to have a good look to see what they were seeing, she had no option but to kick on, keeping Spot's momentum going, but as she swung round towards the straw-bale jump, she saw what could only be Bones and Hoomey coming towards her up the hill from the general direction of the arterial. The horse was covered in sweat but galloping fast and converging on the straw-bale jump, luckily slightly ahead of her. She took a slight pull to avoid disaster, and had a glimpse of Hoomey sitting there pop-eyed, gazing ahead, in his usual trance. Whether he saw her or not she could not tell, but Bones jumped the straw-bales with about six feet to spare and Hoomey landed back in the saddle, having stayed with the horse by his firm grip on the reins, about halfway towards the dreaded slip-rail. Jumping the straw-bales neatly herself, Nutty then saw that Bones was bearing down on the slip-rail with absolutely no intention of stopping, all set for home and the winning-post, and such was his speed and general intimidating approach that leathery Jane was stumbling eagerly backwards towards the shelter of her Mercedes, and the infant Fountains-Abbott sitting inside all poised to start the cassette of 'God Save the Queen' for Spot was so terrified out of his wits that he completely forgot the importance of his task and threw himself under the seat.

By the time Nutty reached the rail and had dismounted and gone through in exemplary fashion, the Fountains-Abbotts were only just emerging from the slit-trenches, shaken and indignant, and Hoomey was out of sight. Nutty hopped back on board without leather Jane recording either her time or who was hidden under the turban, and Spot, much encouraged by the vision of his stable-companion having gone ahead of him, was moving with much more enthusiasm. Nutty rode with the mounting optimism of the captain whose goal seemed now within the bounds of possibility: if Nails had made it, they had three clear rounds between them. What Hoomey had been up to was neither here nor there. He was still alive, which was a distinct bonus, and had done nothing wrong save ride a completely different course from that stipulated by the stewards.

She had forgotten that Jazz's parents were on the course watching, along with Hoomey's and her uncle Knacker and Biddy and Sam Sylvester. She had never seen any of them on her first round and now saw them in a bunch as she approached the gate where she must come to a halt once more. She knew straight away that Gloria's Glamour-Bronze was hardly going to fool Jazz's own mother . . . if only they didn't give the game away in front of the judge!

But no good stopping to explain. She rode past them with her eyes fixed firmly ahead, but was aware of a general dropping of jaws and shrieks of disbelief, and Biddy's special jagged-glass stare which froze from a distance of thirty feet. Eyes down, breathing in her bosom, Nutty negotiated the gate as quickly and delicately as possible, and kicked on furiously, more anxious to get away from her spectators than to make a good time.

But it was a clear, maximum points, and the steward timing her finish never gave her a second glance. She rode straight back to the horse-box where the others were congregated and flung herself off.

'Get changed back quick!' Gloria hissed. 'Before Seb comes nosing!'

'Did Nails get clear? Did you get clear, Nails?'

'Yes.'

'We've beaten them! If you got clear we've done it!'

'Did nobody see you weren't Jazz?'

'His ma did. And Biddy. Here —' Nutty dragged the turban off and shook out her sweaty curls. 'You're welcome, Jazz.'

Jazz was grinning. 'Have you heard? Hoomey rode two miles down the arterial?'

'Not two miles!' Hoomey said indignantly.

'He said he got in the wrong lane and had to go down to the roundabout before he could come back.'

'Hoomey, you never!'

'Bones jumped the fence at the bottom on to the motorway. I couldn't stop him. And over the central reservation.' Hoomey, white and shining, spoke with awe.

'An' you went round the roundabout?'

Hoomey looked embarrassed. 'It seemed best. The traffic was a bit cross. I went right round and back up the proper carriageway. I didn't do anything wrong.'

'Never said that in the rules. On to the arterial, round the round-about and back up the park. You'll be eliminated for Error of Course.'

'But he was wonderful, Nutty! Absolutely wonderful.'

Nutty, having scrubbed her tan off with another bottle of Gloria's never-ending stuff and Midnight's tail-bandage, surfaced as herself and realised that she felt quite fantastic.

'We won!'

'We cheated,' Nails said.

'So did they. It's fair, if you all cheat.'

Nutty looked at Nails again. She worked it out that if he had done a clear, he must be the best scorer, overall, of the day. Jazz had done superb swimming and running scores and a creditable shoot and she had saved the day with her two rides. And Hoomey, having failed in everything, was steeped in wonder at Bones's prowess and wrapped in a dream of delight.

'Which makes us all happy,' Nutty thought, 'Doesn't it?'

Nails didn't show much. He had untacked Switchback and was sponging the sweat off him. Nutty could see parents and teachers converging from one direction and Seb and co from another and knew it was all going to break. She said quietly to Nails, 'Did you have a good ride?'

'Yes,' he said.

None of the adults were coming for him, unless you counted Biddy for her horse. He had never told Stalin what he did. Nobody gave a fig for Nails. But he wasn't kicking the wall any more, or scowling or complaining. In fact he looked at Nutty and *smiled*. Funnily enough, Nutty felt almost as good about that as about winning.

'Anyway you didn't win,' Seb was saying. 'You cheated.'

'Oh, hark who's talking!' Nutty said. 'Who cheated?'

'You rode twice.'

'And who didn't swim, Colin?'

'Prove it. Prove Colin didn't swim.'

'We can't, can we? But we just know. And you prove I rode twice anyway.'

'Anyone could see it was you a mile away, the way you ride.'

'How do I ride then?'

'Like a looney. Only you ride like a looney. And a great big bosom sticking out in front. Who thought you could get away with that?'

'Nobody's disqualified me.'

'We've only got to say, and they'll disqualify you.'

'Okay. And we'll say about Colin not swimming. We'll get Colin to swear on the bible whether he swam or not. And we'll get someone to look at "God Save the Queen" in leathery Jane's Mercedes.'

'Have you all gone mad?' Biddy asked sweetly.

Nutty turned away from Seb and saw all their adult supporters looking at them in a bemused, uncomprehending way, pleased but puzzled. Mr Plumpton was standing in his white trousers with his clean boys, looking rather annoyed.

'Is it true that there's been some cheating somewhere along the line?' he asked Nutty.

'Yes. We've all cheated. So the result should stand.'

'That's damned bad form, I must say. I can't accept that. We shall have to compete again, to settle it.'

Biddy said, 'Just what I was going to say.'

The eight competitors were stunned into silence. Nutty, from her light-headed, glorious state of feeling she was six feet above the ground and still rising, thought of starting the whole business over again and felt herself deflating rapidly like a leaking balloon.

'Again?' she whispered.

'Of course,' the adults said, in a gang. They had had a nice day out and thought the whole thing fine sport and splendid whole-some stuff for the young. Nutty had to sit down. It all floated before her eyes as if she was dying: the early starts, the agony of running and swimming when you were half-dead . . .

'I can't.'

'Why not?'

'I'm a girl. It's against the rules.'

Sam Sylvester, blushing scarlet, said, 'I'm sure, when the school knows what a marvellous performance the four of you have put up today, you will get all the support you need. I can't tell you how impressed I am by what you've done. When the head hears about this – well, I consider it a great day for Hawkwood, whatever the results, to have achieved all that from scratch! And on your own too.'

Biddy cleared her throat ominously. 'Well, not quite –'

'The money – what about the money?' Nutty put in, wanting to get it over.

'Free for winners, I promised. Call it settled.'

'Even counting the cheating?'

'The cheating was all square, as I understand it.'

'But next time, no cheating,' Plumpton put in. 'You agree with me, Sylvester? We'll organize it better next time.'

'I agree.'

'And abide by the rules. No girls,' Nutty said.

'You can be captain though,' Nails said.

'I don't mind being captain.'

'It would never have happened without you.'

The effort it had taken to get Nails committed was probably the greatest of the whole business, and his commitment, Nutty realised, the most rewarding outcome.

'And if we go on doing it,' Hoomey said, 'That means we can keep the horses?'

'Whether you go on or not, there's a home waiting for Bones at my place whenever you want,' Biddy said. 'I never saw a performance like that horse gave today for boldness and –'

'Speed down the arterial, overtaking in the fast lane,' put in Uncle Knacker. 'Police car tried to keep up with 'im and failed!'

How restful show-jumping would be after all this, Nutty thought deliriously! She lay back in the grass and gazed at the shimmering sky. Everyone had been wonderful. The parents were all pleased as punch; Jazz was being chatted up by old Plumpton about swimming in a county team; Biddy was obviously tickled pink with old Bones; Sylvester was all turned on again (and still kept his motor-bike, for Hoomey had never achieved more than nine and a half lengths for all Nails's effort). Uncle Knacker loaded up their horses and Biddy loaded Switchback, and they all piled into their parents' cars to go home.

It was when she was in the stable feeding Midnight that same evening that Nutty realised there was something they had all forgotten, something of such importance that the oversight came to her with a sense of shock. Tired as she was, she put on her plimsolls and set off on what was once, but was now no longer, a training run: more of an amble now, jogging with a long evening shadow tied to her feet, up the long, slow hill to the spire of St Aloysius. She thought he might not be there, flushed out the night before by the police, but Firelight was standing in her favourite corner of the field by the potting shed, and Nails was lying in the grass feeding her crisps out of a packet. Nutty climbed the gate and walked over slowly. The foal Bonfire came to meet her, cheeky and pushy, making her laugh. Nails did not say anything. Nutty went and sat in the grass beside him.

'What you going to do?' she asked.

Nails shrugged.

'You going home to sleep? You don't want to be caught again.'

'No.'

'What then?'

'I'll think of something.' He did not seem much worried.

'It was good today,' Nutty said.

'Yeah. Not bad.'

Nutty wondered if she had misjudged the situation, and wasted her time coming. There was no real evidence to suppose that Nails was much changed. He was leaving school next week, grown-up really. He still didn't seem to care about anything much, in the sense of worrying. When she had asked what he was going to do, she meant about sleeping that night, but when she thought about it again, sitting there, it wasn't only sleeping that night, it was everything. If she was going to worry about Nails, it was hard to know where to start. He was still pretty horrid really, in the sense he was hard to be friends with because he never let any of himself show except when he was cornered, but over the months she had got used to him. And he accepted her; he didn't tell her to beggar off, for instance, which he would have if that was how he felt. But she had no idea what to say, to suggest, now that she had arrived, and she wondered if this captain habit had taken too strong a grip. After all, now it didn't matter a damn to her what Nails did or didn't do. She told herself that, sitting looking at the grass, but she wasn't sure if it was true.

Firelight finished the crisps and Nails lay back in the grass with his eyes shut. Nutty decided to go, but as she got up they both heard a car stop up on the road, and the door slam as someone got out.

'Oh, cripes, don't say it's them again!' Nails sat up abruptly, looking very much as if he cared.

'You can come back with me, if it is.'

'There's no law against sitting here. How can they say anything?'

They both waited anxiously. Someone's head moved along the top of the hedge towards the gate, paused. A woman started climbing over the gate.

'It's Biddy!' Nutty said, amazed.

Nails lay back again with a sigh. 'Thank Christ for that.'

Nutty, having better manners, went to meet her. She was pleased, never having had a chance amongst all their vociferous supporters to speak to her about their satisfactory rides.

'I thought I might find him here, my boy Nails. Did he tell you I'm down as his mother on the police files?'

'His mother! You're not old enough!'

'Now that's exactly the reaction I would have wished to hear. How right you are! Nails, where are you sleeping tonight? As your mother I should know.'

Nails opened his eyes but declined to say anything.

'After all I've done for you, you could at least look interested,' Biddy said, somewhat sharply.

Nails kept his eyes open, as if to show he was that interested.

'I'm all right,' he said.

'I thought, if you don't want to be run in again, and I'm going to get into trouble too if you go on sleeping rough, you could come back with me. I've got an old caravan with a bed in it a groom used to have. There's no one in it now. If you sleep there you can help me with the horses in the morning. We'll each be doing each other a favour. What do you think to that?'

'It's all right, I suppose.'

'I thought it was, myself. In fact, if you make yourself useful, it could become a habit. You could ride exercise for me, and I could give you pocket-money. But you're such a funny little sod, you might not like the idea.'

Nails looked faintly indignant at this.

'Mr Sylvester said you were leaving school next week. It was a surprise to me – I thought you were only thirteen or so.'

Nails scowled.

'But if you're sixteen, well, I could use you.'

Nails sat up.

'Work for you, you mean?'

'Try it. Not if it doesn't work out.'

'Ride an' all?'

'Yes. You did well to get Switchback round today. That was really good riding. I could use a rider like that. And you want a roof over your head, so I gathered this morning.'

'Yeah.'

'Well then?'

'I could try it.'

He did not look entirely convinced, surprisingly.

'I wouldn't get back here much? Not from out where you live, without any transport. What'll happen to –' He hesitated, slightly embarrassed.

'These two you mean?' Biddy scratched Firelight's mane amicably. 'Well, we could have them out on our marshes if Mr Bean is agreeable. They'd do well there.'

Nails released one of his rare smiles.

'That would be okay then.'

'Come on then.'

They walked back up to the gate, the mare and foal following.

'Give you a lift back first, Nutty?' Biddy asked. 'I borrowed my pa's car, for a change. I'm getting too old for motor-bikes, with a son of sixteen.'

'Oh, yes. I'm tired!'

The great cares of her captaincy a thing of the past, Nutty was alseep before the car got home.

24

Hoomey, sated with his parents' admiration and still strung up by memories of his great ride on Bird of Freedom, could not settle down to watch the box, but had to go out, go back to the refrigerator factory, walk on air, alone, to sift over the stupendous feelings of the day. Scorewise, he had failed in everything, but to himself he knew he had not failed.

Bones and Spot had been turned out and were grazing together in the evening sunshine, switching their tails rhythmically at the midges. Hoomey sat on an oildrum and watched, not wanting anything more, just to remember his ride. Arterial and round-about included, it had been pure magic.

Jazz, similarly restless in domestic surroundings, kicked a tin can across the waste ground and came upon Hoomey in his trance, on the oilcan, and sat down on another beside him, grunting acknowledgement. They sat in amicable silence for some time, picking bits of grass to chew, thinking about the day.

'Old Sylvester was surprised,' Hoomey said eventually, and laughed.

'Yeah.'

'His eyes nearly popped out.'

Jazz was remembering Plumpton's invitation, which was the best thing of the day, Plumpton wanting him to join the swim-ming club. Jazz had known his swim was good, had felt it all the way, got into a rhythm and not tired, enjoyed it, had pleased himself. It wasn't much, amongst the whole business, which included chickening out of the ride, but it was good enough to make all the rest seem of little importance, good enough to make his old great grandpa – the one with a spear on the native pony – wink his approval. Jazz felt he had got to know his old great grandpa quite well since he had appeared on the bedside table. There were no tigers to shoot in this life any more, but it didn't mean it was all peanuts. Jazz didn't think today had been peanuts. He'd never have known if he hadn't tried, that he could do a nice thing like that.

'You really think we've got to do it again?' Hoomey asked.

'We done what they wanted. I don't want to ride, but I wouldn't mind doing the other things again.'

'That ride –' Hoomey said. Words failed him.

'Dual carriageway an' all . . . little squirt like you, could be a jockey,' Jazz laughed.

Hoomey didn't laugh. The trance-like look returned to his face. Who said he had no ambition? That's what Sylvester had

170

said, when he'd been to the football match. Well, now he had ambition. After a bit he stood up. It felt good, having ambition.

'Let's go and get some chips, eh?'

They ran all the way, talking as they went, laughing, spring-heeled with resolution. It might all seem different tomorrow. But today, today was all right.